IDENTITY AND
SPATIO-TEMPORAL CONTINUITY

IDENTITY AND SPATIO-TEMPORAL CONTINUITY

BY

David Wiggins

Fellow of New College, Oxford.

BASIL BLACKWELL
OXFORD 1971

Reprinted 1971

ISBN 0 631 103708

PRINTED IN GREAT BRITAIN
BY A. T. BROOME AND SON, 18 ST. CLEMENT'S, OXFORD
AND BOUND BY THE KEMP HALL BINDERY, OXFORD

PREFACE

Most of the material here presented was originally given in lectures at Oxford in Michaelmas Term, 1964. Under the title 'The Absoluteness of Identity' it was submitted in 1965 to an American journal, accepted by that journal, and then delayed by corrections and amplifications which made it much too long for publication in that manner. The text can be read continuously without much reference to the notes, but in many cases the notes are integral to any full defence of the positions taken up.

I have a number of acknowledgments to make, in particular to Professor P. T. Geach, Mr. W. A. Hodges, and Professor B. A. O. Williams. These are spelled out in the notes to the text, but I cannot forbear to make a grateful general acknowledgment of my indebtedness to Williams' own views and writings on this troublesome subject.

D.W.

New College,
Oxford.

CONTENTS

INTRODUCTION

This monograph proposes and attempts to resolve one problem about the notion of identity. The problem is a wholly general one and in the first instance I answer it purely formally. Some defence is offered in 1.2 and 1.7 of the formal principles which I use to get to that answer, but I must emphasize that it is not my intention to offer any complete defence of these principles in this monograph. After two or three indications of the grounds for supposing them to be incontrovertible principles and partially definitive of what we mean by *identical* or *same*, I concern myself almost entirely with their consequences, which are many and complex. In particular, the negative answer to the original question leaves us with a number of interesting problems about the identity of persisting material substances. These are the problems which are then taken up.

Spatio-temporal continuity or coincidence and bodily continuity have regularly figured in recent discussions of such problems as 'What is the principle of individuation?' and 'What is personal identity?'. I think that the notion of spatio-temporal coincidence itself has been assumed to be perfectly clear or quite easy to clarify. That it is clarifiable I am inclined to agree, but the result of clarifying it is not in every case to leave things exactly as they were, or as they seemed to be when the notion was originally imported into these discussions. In Part Four I attempt to give colour to this claim so far as it concerns personal identity.

It gradually became evident to me in constructing this work that for the future of metaphysics no single part of the philosophy of science was in more urgent need of development than the philosophy of biology. It is well known that Aristotle believed something like this but it seems to be the misfortune of that particular philosopher that few of the things he said can be understood or believed until they are laboriously rediscovered. And it is a misfortune of present-day analytical philosophy that it has not inspired the production of any writings in the philosophy of biology which are both worthy to succeed the seminal writings of J. H. Woodger and capable of illuminating present day philosophical discussions of classification and individuation in the way Aristotle would have argued that they require. To this important task I incite those better qualified than I am to undertake it.

ERRATUM

Page 73 *lines* 1—8 *should read:*
(See also fn. 38 and p. 43). If appearance after a temporal gap of suitable object a' could imply or ground the conclusion that $a = a'$ then so would the situation: *appearance of suitable object a' and* p. For $(r \Rightarrow q) \supset (p \ \& \ r \Rightarrow q)$. But what if p assumes the value 'suitable object a'' has also appeared, and $a' \neq a''$'? Sufficient conditions have to be *sufficient* conditions.

It may be objected that all that Williams has shown is that to get a genuinely sufficient condition of identity we must gloss 'suitable appearance of object a'' so that it *simply stipulates* the absence of competitors. 'In addition to suitable object a', suitable object a'' has appeared, and $a' \neq a''$' would then be self-contradictory. For if more than one object appeared after the temporal gap then it would be said by anyone taking this line that neither object was suitable. Hence p could not assume the value 'suitable object a'' has also appeared'.

PART ONE

1.1. *A problem about identity.* *The thesis of the relativity of identity*

Can *a* be the same f as *b* and not the same g as *b*? More precisely, can this happen even when *a* or *b* is itself a g? It is commonly supposed, I think, that it is this sort of possibility which provides the principal grounds for the doctrine, which I shall call D, that, if someone tells you that *a*=*b*, then you should always ask them 'the same *what* as *b*?'[1]

I shall try to show that it cannot be the rationale of D, if D has any rationale, that *a* might be the same f as *b* but not the same g as *b*. Nor, for that matter, can it be derived as a consequence of D. It is not in fact a possibility at all. This matter is treated in Part One. In the following Part, I shall say what I think the rationale of D (limited here to persisting material particulars) really is, and then go on to say something about the purely formal characterization of the notion of a substance or sortal concept.

The doctrine which I shall try to refute in this Part may be more fully stated like this: since there are, or may be, a whole battery of sortal concepts under which a material particular *a* may fall, and under which it may be counted, individuated, and traced through space and time, *a* may coincide with some specified material particular *b* when individuated under some of these sortal concepts and not coincide with *b*, but be wholly distinct from *b*, when individuated under others.[2] So the notion of identity is concept- or sortal-relative, i.e. relative to different possible answers to the question "*a* is the same *what* as b?" I call this R or *the relativisation thesis*.[3] In addition to R and D there will be occasion to mention a further thesis, C, *the counting thesis*, namely this:

> C: to specify the something or other under which *a* and *b* coincide is necessarily to specify a concept f which qualifies as adequate for this purpose, and hence as a *sortal*, only if it yields a *principle of counting* for fs.

It will be my submission that D, R and C are by no means equivalent. D is true.[4] R is false. C is false.[5]

I shall call an individuative or sortal concept which adequately answers the question 'same *what*?' for an identity-statement s, a *covering concept for* s, and reserve the letters f and g to represent such sortal concepts. In the case of an identity '$a=b$' supplemented with covering-concept f, I shall write '$a\underset{f}{=}b$'. The range of ordinary predicate variables, ϕ, ψ, includes both sortal predicates and non-sortal predicates.

The realistic discussion of the relativisation thesis requires not only formal argument but also detailed and in some cases rather lengthy and difficult analysis of examples. For those with little patience or goodwill for the latter kind of activity it will be enough to read section 1.2 below where the principal logical component in the argument is summarized and formalized,[6] and section 3.1 of Part Three where the reasoning of the first two Parts is summarized.

1.2.   *Leibniz' Law and the difficulties of relative identity.*

Plainly the fact that there are many different sortal concepts under which one may trace or individuate an individual a does not straightforwardly imply the possibility of getting different answers to the question whether a coincides or not with some mentioned individual b. For all the alternative procedures of individuation with alternative covering concepts might, when they yielded *any* answer, yield the same answer to that question. My contention is precisely that they must do so. I shall argue that the formal properties of identity provide logically compelling reasons why, where $(\exists f)(a\underset{f}{=}b)$, all different procedures of individuating a (provided they really do individuate a) *must*, if they yield any answer at all, yield the same answer with respect to a's coincidence with b. This is to say that

$$((\exists f)(a\underset{f}{=}b)) \supset ((g)(g(a) \supset a\underset{g}{=}b));$$

which is to say R is false.

Plausible seeming cases of R are hard to find or contrive. I shall try to show exactly how each of the examples I have been able to find or contrive

　　(i) violates the formal properties of identity if construed in a way favourable to R, and

(ii) does not in any case have the logical form which it might seem to have, and which it would need to have to provide an example supporting R.

Although (i) and (ii) overlap they make up essentially distinguishable parts of the consideration of each example.

Under (i) the basic logical difficulty with each supposed example of R is the collision of R with Leibniz' Law. This Law states in its classical unrestricted form that if a is the same as b (or better, if a is the same f as b or $(\exists f)(a \underset{f}{=} b)$), then whatever is true of a is true of b and whatever is true of b is true of a. The most direct way of demonstrating the incompatibility of this Law with R, which says that for some a, b, f and g

$$(a \underset{f}{=} b) \ \& \ (a \underset{g}{\neq} b) \ \& \ (g\,(a)),$$

is to take the ϕ in Leibniz' Law

(1) $(a \underset{f}{=} b) \supset (\phi)\,(\phi a \equiv \phi b)$

as including in its range the predicable '$a \underset{g}{=} x$'. It is extremely important that, as will appear, there are less direct and more satisfying ways of demonstrating the incompatibility than this,[7] but if one does proceed in this direct way then the premiss

(2) $(a \underset{f}{=} b) \ \& \ (g(a))$

can quickly be made to contradict the supposition that $(a \underset{g}{\neq} b)$.

(1) immediately gives

(3) $(\phi)\,((a \underset{f}{=} b) \supset (\phi a \equiv \phi b))$.

Hence with the predicable '$a \underset{g}{=} x$',

(4) $(a \underset{f}{=} b) \supset ((a \underset{g}{=} a) \equiv (a \underset{g}{=} b))$.

But then, by *modus ponens* and the first limb of (2), we can detach the consequent of (4) to get

(5) $(a \underset{g}{=} a) \equiv (a \underset{g}{=} b)$

But by the reflexivity of ' $\underset{g}{=}$ '

(6) $(g\,(a)) \supset (a \underset{g}{=} a)$.

And so by the second limb of (2)

(7) $(a \underset{g}{=} a)$.

Hence, by *modus ponens* with (7) and (5),

(8) $(a \underset{g}{=} b)$.

But this shows that with $(a \underset{f}{=} b)$ & g(a) we can disprove $(a \underset{g}{\neq} b)$ and can thus disprove R.

The second component in the discussion of each apparent example of R is to assign it some other analysis. It will be for the reader to judge whether the distinctions employed in this cause, (ii) above, are independently plausible distinctions. If he thinks they are not plausible, or not independently plausible, or fanciful distinctions, then it is consistent with my short-term intention that he should be led to question the validity of the formal principles which define the traditional concept of identity.[8] That is to say the logicians' concept of identity defined by Leibniz' Law and the principles of transitivity, reflexivity and symmetry. For in this essay my principal objective is simply to indicate the connexion between Leibniz' Law and R (viz. incompatibility) and enlarge our still very imperfect understanding of the *application* of the logicians' notion of identity. I shall draw out some of its implications for the Aristotelian notion of a substance. It is worth being a good deal clearer about what these two notions really are before we defer to the philosophers who would have us discard either of them.

It is not my long term intention, all the same, that this need for distinctions should discredit the classical notion of identity or undermine the formal principles which define it. Their basis seems to me to be *a priori* and incontrovertible, and the concept they define still seems to me, at least when it is properly understood in the light of a correct defence of D, to give the only consistent and clear concept there is either of identity or of substance. And I doubt if we can do without either of these notions. So there may be some point in prefacing a discussion of R with a brief indication of the grounds I think there are for preferring to hold on to Leibniz' Law rather than accept R, or accept any special thesis whatever which conflicts with this law.

If Leibniz' Law were not controverted, I should remark that

it is as obvious as the Law of Non-Contradiction, and simply ask: 'How if *a is b* could there be something true of *the object a* which was untrue of *the object b*? After all, *they are the same object.*' Since it is controverted, I shall add these points:

(i) The principle marks off what is peculiar to identity and differentiates it in a way in which transitivity, symmetry and reflexivity (all shared by *congruence, consanguinity*, etc.) do not.[9]

(ii) The counter-examples to Leibniz' Law are scarcely more impressive than the counter-examples to the Law of Non-Contradiction. There is really something rather extraordinary here in speaking of *counter-examples* at all. Concerning modal and intensional contexts it is still enough, I think, to cite Frege's arguments.[10] His arguments show, and (what is apparently not always understood) they show *quite independently of this issue*, that the apparent reference in intensional and in (some, most or all) modal contexts is not, and *need not have been expected to be*, the actual reference of an expression.

(iii) If Leibniz' Law is dropped then we need some formal principle or other, one of at least comparable universality, to justify the valid instances (if these are not all the instances) of the intersubstitution of identicals. This is a form of argument we cannot simply abandon (whether inside or outside Formal Logic). It is extraordinarily difficult to find or formulate a weaker principle, or amend Leibniz' Law suitably. Some of the difficulties of doing this will be reviewed in 1.7. They add up to a powerful case for the Law.

There is much more to be said about Leibniz' Law, but for the present purpose, which I will describe eirenically as the deline-ation of one concept of identity and one concept of substance, this will be enough. I must now get down to the discussion of R. The discussion is a rather protracted one and the summary at 3.1 and the Table of Contents are intended to help signpost it.

1.3. *Five ways for it to be false that $a \underset{g}{=} b$*

Since what we have to examine is the alleged possibility of a case where $(a \underset{f}{=} b)$ & $(a \underset{g}{\neq} b)$ & $(g(a) \text{ v } g(b))$ it will be as well to proceed on the lines of a routine analysis of the ways in which it

B

is possible for it to be false that $(a \underset{g}{=} b)$. There are five sorts of case:

(1) g may simply be the *wrong* covering concept for both a and b where nevertheless $a = b$. The evening star is the *same planet* but not the *same star* as the morning star. For Venus is not a star. This is not a case of

$$((a \underset{f}{=} b) \ \& \ (a \underset{g}{\neq} b)) \ \& \ (g(a) \ v \ g(b)).$$

(2) Venus is not *the same star* as Mars, nor the same anything as Mars for that matter. For in this case (f) $(a \underset{f}{\neq} b)$. Again this is boring, because we do not have what is needed for the relativisation thesis.

(3) We may seem to get nearer to what is required with the case where John Doe, the boy whom they thought a dunce at school, is the *same human being* as Sir John Doe, the Lord Mayor of London, but not the *same boy* (for the Lord Mayor is not a boy) nor the *same mayor* or *ex-cabinet-minister* or *ex-Minister of Transport* or *father of five marriageable daughters*. (For the boy did not attain office or beget children when a boy.) Yet surely, it may be said, *boy, dunce, mayor, ex-cabinet-minister, father of five marriageable daughters*, are all sortals and all make perfectly good covering concepts. One can count and identify such things, and so on. So this gives the appearance of a case where we have $(a \underset{f}{=} b) \ \&$ $(a \underset{g}{\neq} b) \ \& \ (ga \ v \ gb) \ \& \ (-gb)$, a case in fact where a cuts out, as it were, under a sortal-concept g (e.g. *boy*) but can persist under another sortal-concept f (e.g. *human being*).

I submit that this case is not what the relativist is looking for. All it in fact shows is, first, the necessity for care about tenses, both in the interpretation of the formula—$(a \underset{g}{=} b)$ and in the interpretation of Leibniz' Law; and, second, the possibility of an interesting and highly important distinction within the class of sortal predicates.

If John Doe is still a boy then John Doe, the boy, *will* one day be a cabinet-minister and later the Lord Mayor of London, and he *will* beget five children. If John Doe is no longer a boy, then John Doe the boy (or Sir John Doe, when he was a boy) *was going to be* and *was going to do* these things. We only thought we

had a case of R because we confused the timeless and the tensed way of speaking within one utterance. If 'g(Sir John Doe)' is a tensed statement it should be read as saying that Sir John *was* a boy and it is true. If it is a tenseless statement then it says of Sir John Doe that at some time or other he (timelessly) is a boy. This again is true. If we take tenses seriously it is impossible to say 'Sir John Doe *is* the same boy as John Doe' since it is false that Sir John Doe is now a boy. But it is true and perfectly unproblematic that Sir John Doe *was* the same boy as John Doe. It is precisely for this reason that Sir John Doe is not now standardly individuated under the sortal *boy*. From all this it follows that '$-(a=b)$,' properly read, is not true. We still do not have what
$\quad\quad\quad\text{g}$
the relativist was looking for.

The second matter which type-(3) cases bring to our attention is this. They underline the need to distinguish between sortal concepts which present-tensedly apply to an individual x at every moment throughout x's existence, e.g. *human being*, and those which do not, e.g. *boy*, or *cabinet minister*. It is the former (let us label them, without prejudice, *substance-concepts*) which give the privileged and (unless context makes it otherwise) the most fundamental kind of answer to the question 'what is x?'. It is the latter (one might call them *phase-sortals*) which, if we are not careful about tenses, give a false impression that a can be the same f as b but not the same g as b. In fact they do not conflict at all with what is to be proved: that for all x and all y, every concept which adequately individuates x for any stretch of its existence yields the same answer, *where it does yield any answer at all*, as every other genuinely individuating concept for x or y to the question whether x coincides with y or not.

This brings me to cases of type (4) and (5).

(4) is the variant where, allegedly,

$$(a=b) \ \& \ (a\neq b) \ \& \ (\text{g}(a) \ \text{v} \ \text{g}(b)) \ \& \ (\text{g}(a) \ \& -\text{g}(b)).$$
$\quad\text{f}\quad\quad\quad\text{g}$

(5) is the type of case where, allegedly,

$$(a=b) \ \& \ (a\neq b) \ \& \ (\text{g}(a) \ \text{v} \ \text{g}(b)) \ \& \ (\text{g}(a) \ \& \ \text{g}(b))$$
$\quad\text{f}\quad\quad\quad\text{g}$

We need some examples which might be said to be examples of type (4), and then some for type (5).

1.4 *Possible examples of type-*(4)

(α) I might say to someone 'that heap of fragments there is the jug you saw the last time you came to this house'. They could not be *the same jug* but they might be *the same collection of material bits*.

(β) My visitor might be a person of tiresome ingenuity and glue the pieces of the jug together to make not a jug but, say, a coffee pot of a quite different shape and order of ugliness from the original jug's. It might then be said that 'the jug is the coffee pot' is true with covering concept *same collection of material bits* and false with covering-concept *same utensil*.

(γ) Perhaps the best and least strained example of type (4) is one of a kind which a champion of the relativisation thesis which is stated in P. T. Geach's *Reference and Generality* might describe in the following way:

"Linsky asked in his review of *Reference and Generality*[11] why 'Cleopatra's Needle' could not correspond in use to 'the same landmark' rather than to 'the same (lump of) stone'. And of course it could. For all one knows, 'Cleopatra's Needle' in some people's use does work this way. In that case, if the stone obelisk brought from Egypt corrodes away in the London fogs and is repared with concrete, so that in the end none of the original stone is left, we shall have to say 'The same landmark, namely Cleopatra's Needle, was stone and is concrete'. But now whereas it would be true that Cleopatra's Needle in 1984 is the same *landmark* as Cleopatra's Needle in 1900, it would be false that Cleopatra's Needle in 1984 is the same *stone* as Cleopatra's Needle in 1900—or, indeed, the same stone as anything, since it just wouldn't be a stone in 1984. This gives a case where Cleopatra's Needle is in 1900 both an A and a B, both a stone and a landmark, and goes on being the same B but doesn't go on being the same A.

To take another case, during the Festival of Britain the stone in Meriden, inscribed to show it marks the reputed centre of England, was removed from Meriden to London to be put on show. Such a performance is well within the limits of human folly. Well, during transport it will have remained the same stone but not the same landmark; it is questionable if after its return to Meriden it will be that landmark again—indeed old villagers are alleged to say that it is now some yards off its old site."

These cases, (α) (β) (γ) seem to qualify, if they qualify at all, as cases of type (4) though, with one or two, type-(3) analyses might be essayed.

1.5. *Some cases which might be alleged to be of type* (5).

(δ) An argument in Geach's *Reference and Generality*,[12] might prompt the following suggestion. Whatever is a river is water. Suppose I moor my vessel at the banks of Scamander when that river is in full torrent. The next day, the river on which my vessel is now moored is the *same river* as the river on which I moored it yesterday, but it is not (in spite of the fact that rivers are water) the *same water*. The water in which I moored it is now part of the Aegean.

(ε) John Doe the boy is the *same human being* as Sir John Doe, the Lord Mayor, but not the *same collection of cells* as Sir John Doe.

(ζ) '. . . it may be said, without breach of the propriety of language, that such a church, which was formerly of brick, fell to ruin, and that the parish rebuilt the same church of freestone, and according to modern architecture. Here neither the form nor the materials are the same, nor is there anything in common to the two [*sic*] objects but their relation to the inhabitants of the parish; and yet this alone is sufficient to make us denominate them the same.'[13] So we may say of Hume's church that the present church is the same *church* as the old parish church but not the same *building* or the same *stonework* as the old parish church.

(η) At Paddington Railway Station I point to the Cornish Riviera Express and say 'That is the same train as the train on which the Directors of the Great Western Railway travelled to Plymouth in 1911'. *Same train*, yes, it may be said, but not *the same collection of coaches and locomotive.*

(θ) A petitioner asks to see the same official as she saw last time. The man she sees is the *same official* but not the *same man*.

(ι) The Lord Mayor is not the *same official* as the Managing Director of Gnome Road Engineering Ltd. (indeed they often write one another letters) but he is *one and the same man*.[14]

(κ) Dr. Jekyll and Mr. Hyde were the *same man* but not the *same person* or *personality*.[15]

(λ) 'There is but one living and true God . . . and in unity of this Godhead there be three Persons of one substance, power, and eternity; the Father, the Son, and the Holy Ghost.' (Article

I of the XXXIX Articles). This is to say that the Father, Son and Holy Ghost are the *same God* but not the *same person*.

Some of these examples are better than others but I do not think that any of the examples (a)—(κ) is sufficiently secure to provide an independent argument for the logical possibility of (λ), the most difficult case. So I shall submit that R, the relativisation thesis, is to be rejected.[16]

1.6.   *Discussion of type* (4) *cases*.

(a) and (β) hang together. For if the jug is the same collection of bits as the heap of fragments and the heap of fragments is the same collection of bits as the coffee-pot then, by transitivity, the jug must be the same collection of bits as the coffee-pot. Either both or neither, then, is a true identity-statement. The difficulty is that if the jug is the same collection of material parts, bits of china clay, as the coffee pot, that is if they are one and the same collection of china-bits, then their life-histories and durations must be the same.[17] But the coffee pot *will* be fabricated or assembled at t_3 by my ingenious friend and exist only from then on. The jug won't then exist any more.

(a) will only be what is required as a case of type-(4) if 'that heap is the jug you saw last time' comes to something more than 'the matter you see there is the same matter as the matter of the jug you saw when you came here last time'. Similarly (β) must not simply boil down to the unexceptionable claim that the jug and coffee pot are made of the same matter. Otherwise it is no longer obvious that we have the sort of type-(4) identity-statement the relativist required. To get that, the 'is' of (a) and (β) must take *collection of china-bits* as a straightforward covering-concept and be not comparable to the 'is' in 'the soufflé you are eating is simply eggs and milk' or the 'is' of 'the portico is wood and stucco'. I shall call the latter the 'is' of *constitution*, contrast it with the 'is' of identity, and shall attempt to prove that it is precisely this constitutive 'is' which we have in (a) and (β).

Suppose, with (a), that the jug is the same collection of china bits as the heap of fragments. Then if this is a type-(4) identity statement we are entitled to infer that the jug is (predicatively) a collection of china-bits. (If Hesperus is the same planet as Phosphorus then Hesperus is a planet.) But then there must be some collection of china-bits with which the jug is identical. (For if x is φ then there must be some φ-thing with which x is identical.[18] If Hesperus is a planet then there must be some planet with which Hesperus is identical.) Suppose there were one. Then, again, we have trouble from the principle that if *a* and *b* are identical then they must have the same life history. Suppose I destroy the jug. Do I then destroy the collection? Either I do or I don't. If I do then both (α) and (β) fail of truth with covering concept *collection of china-bits* and fail as type-(4) examples. If I don't thus destroy the collection then it cannot be true of the jug that it *predicatively* is a collection of china-bits. But nevertheless it is *true* that the jug is a collection of china-bits. That is to say that it is china-clay. Therefore it must be true but not straightforwardly *predicatively* true. I suggest that it is true in the sense that the jug is *made of* china clay or *constituted of* a collection of china-bits.[19] But this argument requires two supplementary remarks, one on the behaviour of 'same' in (α) and (β) with the gloss *same collection*, the other on the sense of 'collection'.

The argument is not meant to rely at all on demonstrating the non-identity of jug and collection by insisting on a special or unfair construal of the term 'collection'. In case that is not clear I had better show it. The possible construals seem to be three in number. 'φ (A)' where A is in some sense or other a collection can presumably mean either (i) that class A is φ or, (ii) that each of the As is φ, or (iii) that a *physical aggregate* or concrete *whole*, A, is φ.

Sense (i) cannot be what we are really looking for, even though skilful and opportunistic reinterpretations of φ might hold a set-theoretical interpretation of the 'A' in 'φ(A)' on the rails for an indefinitely long time. In the end the only way in which one could explain breaking or scattering a set-theoretical entity would be parasitic on the way one explained what one had to do to a physical configuration to break or scatter it. At root what we are interested in is a sense of collection or manifold for which there can be no empty or null collection,[20] and for which it holds that 'if we take the German Army as our manifold and an infantry regiment as a domain within it, it is all one whether we choose to regard as elements within it the battalions, the companies, or the single soldiers.'[21] Notoriously this is not true of sets.

Sense (ii) of collection is not what we are looking for here. If I repair or destroy an item I do not repair or destroy each part of it. (Since each part of a part is a part this would be difficult.) Nor in any non-Anaxagorean universe do we wish 'Jug (A)' to mean each of the As is a jug.

Sense (iii) suggests the definition of *sum* or *fusion* in Leśniewski's mereology.[22] An individual X would be a Leśniewskian *sum of* [*all elements* of the class *parts of the*] *jug* J if all [elements of the class] *parts of* J were parts of X and if no part of X were disjoint from all parts of J.[23] This would certainly seem to be the sort of thing we are looking for, because by this method all collections of parts of the jug, however specified (whether as china clay bits or as molecules, or as atoms), and all collections of collections of parts of the jug, etc., are intended to define and exhaust one and the same Leśniewskian whole or sum, X, of the jug. If 'collection' is defined in this way, however, and if mereology is grafted straight onto that pre-existing scheme of three dimensional persisting things which we are operating (and which anybody who wanted to obtain our type-(4) or type-(5) contrasts would have to be willing to operate), then, perhaps, the jug turns out *not* to be the same collection as the coffee-pot in (α) and (β). For if $X = J$ then among the parts of X is J itself. For everything is part of itself. So if J is broken at t_2 and there is no such jug as J after t_2, then it looks as if X does not survive t_2 either.[24]

In fact the problems which would arise in adding mereology to a logical system already possessed of a concept of identity defined for three dimensional continuants have hardly been studied at all, because the adherents of mereology have almost always wished to operate a four dimensional scheme reducing everyday continuants to temporal series of slices, or 'thing-moments', of spatio-temporal regions of the space-time continuum.[25] They make a radical distinction, therefore, between identity or difference *at* a time and identity or difference *through* time. For the former concept '$x = y$' can be defined mereologically by the condition that x is a part of y and y is a part of x; whereas for spatio-temporal continuity (or what is sometimes called *genidentity*) these definitions have to be supplanted or supplemented by special conditions of a quite different character. What matters here, in a discussion of (α) and (β), is that however these extra conditions be stated, whatever alternatives there may be to Leśniewski's general method of defining 'concrete collection', and however three-dimensional wholes are accommodated, there remains the same fundamental dilemma. Either 'concrete collection' is defined in such a way that concrete collection X has the same principle of individuation as the jug or it is not so defined. If it is not, then the life-histories principle debars X from identity with the jug and the type-(4) example disappears.[26] But if X does have the same principle of individuation as the jug then again, for a different reason, we don't have a type-(4) example. For under this option the jug then isn't the same concrete collection as the coffee-pot. What is more, the chances are that the whole project of equating thing and matter will then have degenerated into triviality. If X is to be defined so as to be no more and no less tolerant of damage, replacement of parts etc., than the jug then we shall virtually have to steal the concept *jug* so as to secure the right configuration and persistence-conditions for X. But this is to ascend from the level of bits of things to the level of something whole, structured, and jug-like, namely a jug. The jug is *constituted of* certain matter and identical only with a certain *whole* or *continuant* at present constituted in a certain way out of that matter. That is to say with the jug. Unless the project is thus trivialized and concrete collection so defined, the true statement that the jug or the coffee pot *is* X must not be allowed by anybody who accepts the life histories principle to have the standard consequence of predicative 'is' that it is *identical* with X. The 'is' must mean 'is constituted of', and *collection of parts* will not function standardly as a normal covering concept in either (α) or (β).

Since 'the jug is the heap of fragments' and 'the jug was the same china-clay as the coffee pot' both boil down to identity of *matter*, the supplementary remark about 'the same' which was promised on page 11 is simply this, that 'the same' can do appropriate duty with this constitutive 'is' just as readily as it can do duty with '=' (where it yields so called numerical identity—'is the *same substance* or *continuant* as') and with predicative 'is' (where it yields so called qualitative identity—'is qualified by some *same predicate* as'). So much for (α) and (β).

Example (γ) also requires considerable unpacking, but I think its power to convince is quite deceptive. We may begin by asking what is *meant* by 'Cleopatra's Needle'—what it is that someone points to when they point to Cleopatra's needle. There is here a special difficulty which has to be faced by a consistent defender of the position Geach took up in *Reference and Generality*. To keep example (γ) in play at all as a type-(4) example the defender will have to claim that *landmark* and *stone* give different principles of identity. But by the theory of proper names defended in *Reference and Generality*, the sense of a proper name is given by the principle of identity built into the general term associated with it. It seems to follow that if 'Cleopatra's Needle' had two equally good but different 'nominal essences' then it ought to be ambiguous. In which case (γ) should not surprise or impress us any more than any startling paradox arrived at by equivocation.

Rather than object in general to this theory of proper names,[27] let us simply examine the different specifications one might give of the meaning of 'Cleopatra's Needle'. What is Cleopatra's Needle? What substance is it? Is it a stone? If a stone is what it (substantially and predicatively) is, then surely when that stone is rotted away completely Cleopatra's Needle is rotted away completely. For they are one and the same stone. Cleopatra's Needle, the stone, is not then the same *anything* as anything which exists in 1984. For if that stone, Cleopatra's Needle, no longer exists in 1984 then it is not the same landmark then as anything in 1984, though something quite different may have come to fulfil the same role as it did.

But perhaps the fact the stone has completely rotted away by 1970 does not imply that there is no longer any such thing as Cleopatra's Needle. *Stone* is not then the sense-giving sortal. It may be that *monument* or *monument suitable for use as a landmark* is what Cleopatra's Needle substantially is. And perhaps monuments can be completely refashioned and still persist. But then 'Cleopatra's Needle in 1984 is not the same stone as Cleopatra's Needle in 1900' need only mean that Cleopatra's Needle is not *made of the same material* as it was in 1900. The dates surely qualify the verb in any case. Once its matter was a (piece of) stone, now its matter is concrete. In that case the words 'the same' are serving in (γ), with the versatility already remarked upon à propos of (α) and (β), to indicate that you can't say about the *material* of Cleopatra's Needle in 1984 what you could have said in 1900. (A type-(3) analysis may be possible too.)

These are not all the possibilities. One might think *landmark* was what gave 'Cleopatra's Needle' its sense. But there is in fact something rather peculiar about treating the sortal 'landmark' as an ordinary substance-concept suitable for giving a proper name a sense. It is really more like a title conferred on an object when it secures a certain position of a certain conspicuousness, almost like 'chairman' or 'official' or 'president' or 'sovereign'; in which case, in one use, it is a qualification of a sortal and itself presupposes an underlying sortal which says what *sort* of object. This takes us back to the possibilities already mentioned. There does however exist the possibility of another use, which one might call a *titular* use, of the phrase 'same landmark'. According to this, for *x* to be the same landmark as *y*, *x* has simply to mark the same spot as *y* did. If this use exists then it is possible to say in similar manner that Lyndon Johnson is the same official as John F. Kennedy (to wit, President of the United States); and, similarly, all that is required for Elizabeth II to be the same Queen as Elizabeth I is that she should be sovereign of the same country.[28] But of course in this use *something else*, something non-identical with the obelisk and distinct under every genuine covering-concept, can succeed it as the same landmark. It must be this view of 'landmark' which (γ)'s defender exploits in suggesting that the Meriden stone ceases to be the same landmark when it is transported to London. 'Cleopatra's Needle' then turns out not to be an ordinary proper name at all but to be an abbreviation for the description 'whatever suitable object of suitable dignity conspicuously marks such and such a spot on the Embankment in London'.

The effectiveness of this critique of example (γ) does not depend on there being a hard and fast or canonically correct answer to the question 'what is Cleopatra's Needle?'. The example may owe a specious plausibility precisely to the fact that 'Cleopatra's Needle' can sustain itself indefinitely long ambiguously poised between these and perhaps yet other incompatible senses.

So much for the alleged cases of (4). In fact it begins to appear why there simply *cannot* be cases of type-(4). Where

$(\exists f)(a \underset{f}{=} b)$ and allegedly $(\exists g)\,(a \underset{g}{\neq} b)$ and g(a) v g(b) either g is a substantial sortal or it is not. If it is not substantial then it will always need to be proved that we have more than a type-(3) case or a case of constitutive 'is'. If it is a substantial sortal then either a or b has to be a g without the other being a g. But this violates Leibniz' Law. The objection will not necessarily apply in quite this form to alleged cases of type-(5), to which we now come.

1.7. *Discussion of type-(5) cases and some attempted amendments of Leibniz' Law.*

The identity-interpretation of (δ) and Leibniz' Law are incompatible. Unlike the water, the river on which I moored my boat yesterday is not a part of the Aegean. Rivers are indeed water but this means that water goes to make them up. 'Same water' is not therefore a covering concept for an identity statement identifying a river with something.[29]

(ϵ) is fairly easily unmasked. If 'collection of cells' will do as covering concept, and if 'is a collection of cells' doesn't merely mean 'is made up of cells', then John Doe must be identical with some definite collection of cells, which will have to share all properties of John Doe. *What* collection of cells? Suppose we make 'collection of cells' mean 'such and such aggregate' (with fixed constituents). But then one aggregate is succeeded by another. John Doe is not similarly succeeded. One aggregate is dissipated. John Doe isn't. But then 'John Doe is such and such collection of cells' has to have the constitutive interpretation. (Compare (α) and (β)). Suppose we make 'collection of cells' mean 'aggregate with a succession of constituents through time'. We then no longer have an example of type-(5) at all, change of truth-grounds by change of covering concept. For in this sense man and boy are the same aggregate of cells.

(ζ) resembles (γ) in a certain specious exploitation of ambiguities. Hume goes on in tell-tale manner to say 'But we must observe, that in these cases the first object [sic] is in a manner annihilated before the second comes into existence; by which means, we are never presented, in any point of time, with the idea of difference and multiplicity; and for that reason are less scrupulous in calling them the same'. Hume has less interest than we ought to have in pressing the point I am about to make because, having distinguished respectable strict 'numerical' identity from what he variously dubs 'imperfect', 'specific', 'fictitious' identity (the lamentable ancestor, I suppose, of 'genidentity', and a notion which on one occasion he even calls a perfect notion of *diversity*!), he can then afford to let you say whatever you please about the rather disreputable second notion. But we must insist—*either* we make up our minds to say the building was annihilated *or* we do not make up our minds so.

If we do say the building was annihilated then a certain building seems to be found in existence after it lapsed from existence. It is easy to avoid this absurdity. In 'The present church is the same church as the old church', either (i) 'church' in the second of its three occurrences does not mean 'building' but what can persist when a congregation loses its church-building (in which case the constitutive 'is' comes near to signifying something like 'houses' or 'embodies', and there is a zeugma when we say the present church (i.e. church-*building*) is *not* the same building as the old), or (ii) 'church' means 'building' all right in its first and third occurrences but behaves in the titular fashion and unlike a proper covering-concept at its second occurrence, as it was supposed 'land mark' might behave in (γ) (meaning say 'whatever building houses such and such a congregation"). Either way we lose the type-(5) identity-statement.

If we do not make up our minds to say that the church was annihilated then either we do not know what to say about the example, or we say that it was not annihilated. It is then false that the new church is not the same building as the old one. It is the same, and has simply been repaired and remodelled. That is what we have decided to say.

Again the rebuttal does not depend on its being a hard and fast question how 'church' behaves in the example. As before, the example cannot survive by poising itself ambiguously between mutually exclusive alternatives.

In (η) the appearance of a type-(5) case relies entirely on the failure to say what is meant by 'Cornish Riviera Express'. Once this is specified no ambiguity remains at all. Manifestly, to admit the possibility of an express surviving its present coaches and locomotive is to admit its non-identity with these. But then *collection of coaches and locomotive* is a non-starter for straightforward covering concept, and we have a constitutive 'is'. (Alternatively perhaps we have a titular use of 'same train' or 'same express'.)

(θ) is equally easily exposed. Suppose official *a* is succeeded by official *b*. The petitioner therefore sees *b* on her second visit. She doesn't see the same office-holder but the holder of the same office, *whoever he is*. '*a* is the same official as *b*' doesn't ascribe 'numerical identity' to *a* and *b* at all. It *predicates* something of them in common, holding a certain office. In *the same's* extensive repertoire this is one of the better known roles. Cp. *landmark*.

(ι) exploits an ambiguity. Under one interpretation it is simply false. In fact Sir John Doe, that tireless official, is both Lord Mayor and Managing Director of Gnome Road Engineering. So they *are* one and the same official. The interpretation which makes the first part of (ι) true concerns *what it is to be Lord Mayor* and *what it is to be Managing Director of Gnome Road Engineering*. These Frege would have called concepts. And what (ι) then says is that to satisfy the one concept, have the one office, is not necessarily to satisfy the other, have the other office. (That is to say that, appearances perhaps to the contrary, the two offices are not tied and that Gnome Engineering do not actually nominate the Lord Mayor). To add 'they are the same man' and 'they often write one another letters' is to exploit the possibility of understanding 'they' the second time round, as 'the man who satisfies this concept and the man who satisfies that concept.' 'They' has to be read differently in different parts of (ι) and there is an inoffensive zeugma.

(κ) touches on large issues. Certainly neither *human being* nor *homo sapiens* is synonymous with *person*, but this does not prove the point. And the difficulty is this. If Mr. Hyde visited Tilbury Docks at 9.30 p.m. on December 18th, 1887, then Dr. Jekyll did too. Leibniz' Law would have to be drastically amended to avoid this consequence of their being the same man. And the same applies to whatever Mr. Hyde did at Tilbury Docks. By Leibniz' Law Dr. Jekyll will have done the same. Now Dr. Jekyll the man is a person and he did these things at Tilbury Docks. But then is he not the person who did these things at the docks? How then can he be a different person from Mr. Hyde? The only way to make (κ) even come out true is to give it a rather odd and implausible interpretation and interpret it to mean that to satisfy the concept *identical with Dr. Jekyll* (or *man* who is ϕ, ϕ') is not necessarily to satisfy the concept *identical with Mr. Hyde* (or *man* who is ψ, ψ'), and so to have such and such personal characteristics is not necessarily to have such and such other personal characteristics. Contingently, though, to satisfy the one concept was (in R. L. Stevenson's story) to satisfy the other. 'Dr. Jekyll' and 'Mr. Hyde' have then to be read twice over in (κ) to make it come out true, first as standing each for a man (this individual is the same man as that individual) the second time as standing for a certain kind of character or personality. (These personalities, not these men, are different.) But the example really represents an implausible attempt to postulate (philosophically full-blooded) schizophrenia without going the whole way and postulating two men (sharing one body) as well as two persons.

This brings me to (λ), and to what is perhaps overdue, a reexamination of Leibniz' Law. I cannot hope to exhaust all the theological implications or examine every possible formulation but the plain difficulty is that if the Son who was God was crucified and was the same God as the Father then according to Leibniz' Law unamended the Father was crucified. I believe this involves one in the heresy of *patripassionism*. If so, it was understandable that the Church Fathers condemned Noetus and his followers, who, it seems, believed this. For one application of Leibniz' Law is as good as any other and if the Fathers of the Church had allowed the Patripassiani their way, then the three Persons, Father, Son and Holy Ghost, would have been in danger of collapsing into one another. For, in exactly the same way, all the predicates of Christ which applied uniquely to him or applied to him at a time and place will have applied to the Father and Holy Ghost; and one would not need the full dress Identity of Indiscernibles

$$(\phi) (\phi(a) \equiv \phi(b)) \supset (a = b),$$

where ϕ is restricted to genuine predicates,[30] but only the obviously true principle which results from lifting all restrictions on the range of ϕ and admitting impure predicates with imbedded proper names, in order to prove heretically that Son, Father and Holy Ghost coincided at a place and time under the concept *person* as well as coinciding, presumably in some other way, under the concept *God*.

The difficulty for the relevant formulations of the doctrines of the Trinity and Incarnation, and for all purported cases of type-(5), is this. The truth of D (see Part Two page 34) is certainly a good philosophical motive for enriching the identity-calculus with sortal and substantial-sortal variables and for restating the familiar laws in a restricted form. Transitivity would be restated and restricted as

$$(f) \ (x) \ (y) \ (z) \ ((x \underset{f}{=} y \ \& \ y \underset{f}{=} z) \supset (x \underset{f}{=} z)),$$

and similarly symmetry and reflexivity. But the whole project turns out to be pointless, and cases of type-(5) turn out to be impossible, if the resulting calculus collapses into the unrestricted calculus. Yet this is precisely what happens, of course, if Leibniz' Law remains in its familiar form. For suppose we are told that $(a \underset{f}{=} b)$. Then for any ϕ, ϕ is true of a if and only if it is true of b. Amongst ϕ will be individuating characteristics of a, e.g. uniquely identifying predicates such as 'begotten of the Father' and spatio-temporally identificatory attributes, ψ, of a. So if and only if a is ψ, b is ψ. But now for any substantial sortal g, if and only if a is a g then b is a g. And it must be the same g, namely the one that is ψ. But then we can *deduce* all the unrestricted principles.

The only thing, then, which an upholder of (λ) who insisted on interpreting it as an identity statement could do would be to amend or restrict Leibniz' Law. If the law is to play anything at all similar to its present indispensable role, the justification of the intersubstitution of identicals, then for any a and b such that $(\exists f)$ $(a \underset{f}{=} b)$, there must be *some* condition under which the amended law allows us to draw the conclusion that ϕb from the premiss that ϕa. What condition?

The amended law might read:

LL.I: $((f) \ ((f(a) \ v \ f \ (b)) \supset a \underset{f}{=} b)) \supset ((a \underset{g}{=} b) \supset (\phi)(\phi(a) \equiv \phi(b)))$

This restriction would certainly save example (λ). It does so more or less by legislation. But how on earth does one ever establish that $((f) \ (f(a) \ v \ f(b)) \supset (a \underset{f}{=} b))$? By establishing that a and b have all their properties in common? But this was what was precisely at issue over the Father and the Son and the predicate 'is the same person'. And we normally establish community of properties, anyway in the specially favourable case against which we understand the other cases, by finding that a and b spatio-temporally coincide under a concept and then invoking Leibniz' Law to *deduce* the truth of various tensed propositions about a from tensed propositions about b. But this is precisely what we cannot do in the case where all we have is LL.I. It gives a permission to intersubstitute identicals which can never, from the nature of the case, be taken up at all.

A method of dispensing with Leibniz' Law which I have had occasion to discuss with Mr. W. A. Hodges is to try to make do with this property of ' $=\limits_f$ ',

LL.II: $(a \underset{f}{=} b) \supset (\phi)[(x)(x \underset{f}{=} a \supset (\phi x)) \equiv (y)(y \underset{f}{=} b \supset (\phi y)]$

The principle is unquestionable on any view, though it might be thought an objection to the project of making it do duty for Leibniz' Law that the identity-sign would then have to figure in what would then have to serve as a partial *elucidation* of the notion of identity. Waive this for a moment, and this second manoeuvre may perhaps preserve (μ). But the trouble is that the device by itself gives us too little and we are left without guidance for the rest of what we need. Suppose we know that

(1) Cicero $\underset{man}{=}$ Tully

and that

(2) ϕ (Cicero) ($=$ Cicero denounced Catiline)

Then by *modus ponens*, and universal instantiation it follows that

(3) (x) $(x \underset{man}{=} \text{Cicero} \supset \phi(x)) \equiv (y)$ $(y \underset{man}{=} \text{Tully} \supset \phi(y))$

But to get anything more interesting than (3) we need something which cannot be regarded as logical truth when unrestricted Leibniz' Law is withdrawn, namely,

(4) (x) $(x \underset{man}{=} \text{Cicero} \supset x$ denounced Catiline)

Now provided we know (4) to be true—and LL.II gives us no guidance at all about whether it is true or not —, then (1) and universal instantiation and *modus ponens* give us *directly*

C

(5) Tully denounced Catiline.

It is (4) which does all the work, and we need to be told on what principles, in the absence of the unamended Law, we are to decide the truth of propositions which link particulars and attributes in the way in which (4) links *man*, Cicero and *denounced*. Why is there no similar true proposition leading to a similar deduction with the subjects The Father and The Son and the predicate *was crucified at such and such a time and place*? The answer must be that the connexion which holds between *man*, Cicero, Tully, and *denounced* and makes (4) true does not hold between *God*, the Father, The Son, and *crucified at such and such a time and place*. It might be said, as Hodges put it, that *crucified* does not *transfer over* the concept God. But now one wants to ask, why not? Surely, since the intersubstitution of identicals is a logical procedure, we are entitled to some general principles or other which will at least tell us how to start considering such questions, and tell us what counts as a consideration for and against such propositions as (4). It may be said that crucifixion is a thing which can only be done to a person with a body, and the Father has not a body. But this depends on his connexion with the Son. One cannot rule that he has not a body unless there is a clear way of blocking the *inference* from Christ's having a body to the Father's having a body. By what acceptable principle is it blocked? Moreover, if the Father has not a body is the predicate *person* univocal in its application to the Father and the Son? They are two *what*? If this question cannot be answered then how can we be satisfied that Father and Son are not in different categories? If they were in different categories then how could they be the same God? And surely 'God' has to be univocal, if they are to be the same God.

The same question becomes more immediately important for our purposes—amongst which I do not here number attempting to refute (λ) under all interpretations, only refuting it as an identity-statement with any independent leverage in the larger dispute—if we ask how the predicate *God who was crucified* can fail to transfer over the concept *God*. Yet surely if Christ is God and was crucified then he is God who was crucified.[31] He can't very well be a different God who was crucified from the Father.

One way to block the latter inference to 'Christ is (the) God who was crucified' is to deny that it was *qua God* that Christ had a body or was crucified.[32] But if this escape is used then there is a simpler amendment to Leibniz' Law, which will do everything we have been asking for:

LL.III: $(a \underset{f}{=} b) \supset (\phi(a)$ as an $f \equiv \phi(b)$ as an $f)$

This amendment has also the advantage—not shared by any other amendment which I have been able to think of—of indicating how f and ϕ would have to be related to secure a valid application of the intersubstitution of identicals. It seems to promise that it will tell us something about how to evaluate such propositions as (4) above and make a start in deciding questions of transferability. I shall not press the special difficulties of seeing how on any view resting on the non-transferability of *crucified* with respect to *God* it would be possible for Christ the God to be the same anything as Christ the person who was crucified, or try to devise embarrassing questions about the complex predicate 'was, *qua* God incarnated, *qua* person crucified'. I pass to some general difficulties in making the required sort of sense of *qua* or *as*.

We are now to suppose that there is no other substitutivity-principle than the amended Leibniz' Law, that the proposed restriction is a completely general one, and that a predicate ϕ will only transfer between terms if it can be related in the right way to an f (present or readily available) under which the terms coincide as the same f. Now there are undoubtedly places where *qua* or *as* or similar devices occur essentially, and where an individual a has to be characterized (ϕa as an f) and (not-ϕa as a g). But I shall submit that this is a circumscribed and special phenomenon.

(1) It may arise with what have been called *attributive* adjectives such as *big, small, tall, short, real, good, bad*. Thus a ship can be big for a destroyer and small for a cruiser, a man tall for a Japanese but short compared with most Americans, a picture a real Van Meegheren and not a real Vermeer, a wooden duck a real decoy duck but not a real duck, a witticism a good joke but not a good thing to say at that particular moment.

(2) There can be reference via *qua* or *as* to a rôle which a thing or a man plays: As a general he was obliged to be present at the Court Martial, as the best marksman in the regiment not; as a

socialist he was well placed to protest, as a member of Mr. Harold Wilson's government, hardly; Sir John Doe sent the letter as Managing Director (i.e. in the course of his duties for Gnome Engineering), not as Lord Mayor.

(3) *Oratio obliqua* and straightforward referential opacity can also take cover under *as* or *qua*: x sent the letter to Sir John Doe as Lord Mayor not as Managing Director (i.e. x *addressed* or *directed* the letter 'The Lord Mayor'); Philip, who does not know that Cicero is Tully, may believe Cicero, as Cicero but not as Tully, (or believe Tully, as Cicero but not as Tully) to have denounced Catiline (i.e. think of him under this name rather than that).

What the present proposal seeks to do, however, is utterly to generalize this phenomenon, without doing anything to show us how to find a '*qua* f' for every ϕ, or how to decide the applicability or meaning of every such composite predicate. At greater length a rather more exhaustive and exact typology of *qua* and its congeners could have been devised,[33] but what is certain is that *qua* is not ubiquitous in its operation to produce these or comparable effects. Not every adjective has an attributive use. Individuals are many things (satisfy many predicates) otherwise than by virtue of playing of some rôle or other. Referential opacity is not to be found absolutely everywhere. Moreover it is certain that *qua* does not always produce a single kind of effect for which a unitary rule of the proposed kind could be laid down. (Consider the difference that, with certain precautions, 'qua f' is removable *salva veritate* from affirmative 'ϕ *qua* f' in kinds (2) and (3) and not so removable in kind (1).)

It would seem that the general trouble with the whole proposal is that if the amended law states a condition which legitimates only the transfer of predicates of such kinds as (1), (2) and (3), i.e. predicates which can be got naturally into a *qua* formulation, then (i) it arbitrarily rules out any transfer of other predicates; and (ii) it seems pointless because it suggests that the unamended Law is perfectly all right for transfer from proper name to proper name provided that we do something which was always surely envisaged, transfer the '*qua* f' as well as the 'ϕ'. On the other hand, if it is indeed a completely general proposal affecting all predicates then (iii) vicious regress will have to be guarded against;[34] (iv) for some ϕ it will be unclear what occurrences of 'ϕ *qua* f' even mean, unclear how this contrasts with '*qua* g', and unproven that one would always find what gives the phenomenon its only relevance or interest in this connexion, viz. that $(\exists f)(\exists g)$ $((\phi a$ as an f) $\&-(\phi a$ as a g$))$; and again, (v), it seems pointless for the same reason as (ii) above.

In default then of any adequate amendment of Leibniz' Law I hold onto the unamended Law, of which I sketched a defence in section 1 of this Part. Certainly examples $(a) - (\lambda)$ are incompatible with it when read as identity-statements. I have suggested that there are other, independently plausible, ways of reading $(a)-(\kappa)$. (λ) I leave on one side.

1.8 *A mathematical example supposedly of type* (5).

This monograph is not directly concerned with abstract entities but since the arguments which have been used against examples $(a)—(\lambda)$ have been formal arguments they should not fall foul of mathematical or logical examples of this sort.

(μ) Suppose we have a relation R which holds only between *a* and *b* and between *c* and *d*. Then the relation R in extension may be said to be the set $\{ <a, b>, <c, d> \}$, i.e. the set whose members are the ordered pairs $<a, b>$ and $<c, d>$. Now there are a number of different and equally allowable definitions of an ordered pair. For example, $<x, y>$ can be defined either as $\{\{x\},\{x,y\}\}$ or as $\{\{x\},\{ \wedge, y\}\}$. One might then say (from the *extrasystematic* point of view) that the set S, namely $\{\{\{a\}, \{ \wedge, b\}\}, \{\{c\},\{ \wedge, d\}\}\}$, was *the same relation* as set S', namely $\{\{\{a\},\{a, b\}\}, \{\{c\},\{c, d\}\}\}$. But it is certainly not *the same set* as S'.

As usual the objection to accepting this apparent type (5) example at its face-value is Leibniz' Law. If S=S' under the concept *relation* then whatever is true of S is true of S' and *vice versa*. But S has $\{\{a\} \{ \wedge, b\}\}$ as a member and S' does not.

Notice that any project of saving (μ) by some amendment of Leibniz' Law plus some doctrine or other of categories is more than usually evidently hopeless. Suppose we say that we can only expect what is true of S *qua relation* to be true of S'. Well, either relations are or they are not sets. If they are sets then the plea is absurd, R is a set like S and S' and we still have the violation of Leibniz' Law. If they are not sets, however, then the true statement 'set S is the same relation as S'' must not be allowed to have the consequence that S or S' (predicatively) is a relation. We must only allow, when we are looking at this question extra-systematically, that it *represents* a relation. But to block this consequence is to withdraw (μ) as a genuine case of type–(5). If we want a reduction of relations of degree n which strictly equates them with something then we shall have to isolate and utilize what it is that all mathematically satisfactory definitions of ordered n-tuples have in common.

If we do block the unwelcome consequences of (μ) (rather than vainly try to settle which is 'the right definition' of ordered pair) then what sort of 'is' do we have in (μ)? Presumably it is analogous to the 'is' of 'Irving is Hamlet' or the 'be' of 'that piece of sugar can be your queen [at chess] while I glue the head of the queen back on'. It may be that the 'identifications' of the reduction of arithmetic to set-theory have to be similarly explained. One could dub this 'the "is" of reduction',[35] provided one did not think either that such a name explained anything, or that any *one* explanation of reductive 'is' was possible. It depends on the reduction.

PART TWO

2. *The Rationale of the 'Same What?' Question. Towards a Formal Theory of Substances*

If R, the relativisation thesis, had been correct then it would have given very good support to D, the doctrine that, on pain of indefiniteness, every identity statement stands in radical need of the answer to the question *same what?* For if R had been true it would have followed immediately that there was a serious indeterminacy in the truth-grounds of an uncompleted and unexplained identity-statement, '$a=b$'. Although R could hardly have precluded the possibility of reading '$a=b$' as 'a and b are the same something' or '$(\exists f)(a \underset{f}{=} b)$', it would certainly have shown there was something radically wrong with any putative assertion of identity for which *in principle* no such answer could be provided.

Since contention R is false and since it therefore lends no support to D, we need to know what the rationale of D, if it has one, really is. Confining the discussion more strictly to the identity of persisting material things, I shall first show that D reflects a truth of logic, then go behind this truth of logic to show how crucially D enters into the explanation of the truth-grounds of any statement of identity between material individuals.

If $a=b$, then there must be such a thing as a. In that case there must be something or other which a is. Now, since existence is not a predicate, 'an existent' does not answer the question 'what is a?' Yet since everything is something, this is a question to which there must *be* some answer, known or unknown, if there is indeed such a thing as a. But since a substantial or sortal predicate is by definition no more than the sort of predicate which answers this kind of question, there must automatically exist a sortal predicate f which a satisfies and some sortal predicate g which b satisfies, if a and b exist. Now if in fact $a=b$, then by Leibniz' Law whatever a satisfies b satisfies. So they share all sortal predicates which either of them satisfies. But then if it has any point or makes any sense at all to speak of a and b being the same something or other, of their being the same f, it must make sense to speak of the particular f which both a and b are. By Leibniz' Law, and by transitivity, it must be the same one. So $(a=b) \supset (\exists f) \, (a \underset{f}{=} b)$.

This is all right so far as it goes. Abstractly and schematically, we see that D is a sort of tautology. But so far everything depends on the anterior acceptability and point of the locution 'a is the same f as b' and its implication that a and b are f's. We also need to see why it is logically prior to 'a is an f, b is an f, and $a=b$'. To get any real insight into the matter and go behind this rather misleading demonstration it is necessary first to strengthen this result a little, then to explain the strengthened version's rôle in the theory of individuation, and to draw out the rather stringent conditions it imposes on any general term or sortal f purporting to be adequate to say what a and b sortally or substantially are.

Strawson's notion of sortal-concept descends directly from Aristotle's notion of *second substance*. Aristotle distinguished the category of *substance* from the category of *quality* by contrasting the question *what is X?* with the question *what is X like?* But, as he recognized, this is hardly more than a way of drawing attention to an intuitive distinction; and it is a distinction which it is possible to feel and in practice recognize without having the slightest idea of how to make it properly clear or how to guard it against a scepticism akin to various positions defended at one time and another by such philosophers as F. P. Ramsey and A. J. Ayer. Aristotle's further explanations of his distinction, like almost everything he said about *ousia*, are of such obscurity that they have virtually to be reinvented in order to be interpreted. Nevertheless there are grammatical criteria (that substance-words or sortals admit the definite and indefinite articles, that they form plurals, that it makes no sense to ask *tree what?* and does make sense to ask *blue what?* and so on) which make one suspect that there must be something defensible and clarifiable in that distinction between noun and adjective which subsequent philosophers have tried to hit off by calling the former *individuative, articulative, boundary-drawing, classificatory* terms, terms which *divide their reference*, or (not quite correctly, see p. 39 below) terms which *give a principle of counting or enumeration*. But none of these ideas, articulating, classifying, drawing boundaries, counting and so on, is quite correct enough, or alternatively quite independent enough of the notion of an *individual* or *object*, to bear the weight which has to be borne by an orthodox definition. We can only echo Frege's remark 'the question arises what it is that we are calling an object. I regard a regular definition as impossible, since we have here something too simple [and one might add, too general] to admit of logical analysis'.[36] But neither this, nor the fact that to generalize the sortal *man* into *animal* and this into *object* is to pass over into a mere stencil or dummy-sortal with no vestige of classificatory purport, is ground for total despair. If the general notion of a sortal is a purely formal notion we may at least be able to provide formal criteria for being a sortal.

One of the clear facts about sortal concepts is that as a matter of fact they are used to cover identity-statements. To see why this is and has to be so, and what its consequences are, may be to provide us with some of the materials one would require to elucidate the notion of a sortal or substance-concept. This will be my approach. But it is essential to recognize from the start, and freely admit, that its answer to scepticism is exceedingly indirect. For it requires one provisionally to accept and continually to use the notions of *substance* and *same substance* in order to elucidate and vindicate the conditions of their application.

It is a mark of faith in a more than grammatical distinction between noun and adjective to embrace thesis D. Indeed those who have upheld D have generally believed that there is always to be discovered not merely what we have called a *phase-sortal* but also what we have called a *substance-concept* appropriate to cover any identity-statement. It is important to see that we have not yet done anything at all to justify this belief. The principle we employed above, that everything is something or other, only amounted to the assertion that for all times *t* at which *a* exists, there is a g which *a* is at *t*; or more perspicuously

(D.i): $(x)\,(t)\,[(x \text{ exists at } t) \supset (\exists g)\,(g\,(x) \text{ at } t.)]$

All this guarantees is a *succession* of possibly different phase sortals for every continuant. It does not guarantee that there will be any one or any set of preferred sortal-concepts which a thing will fall under *throughout* its existence. To secure the truth of D for substance-sortals we first require the harder proposition

(D. ii): $(x) (\exists g) (t) [(x \text{ exists at } t) \supset (g (x) \text{ at } t)]$
This principle certainly does not flow from the fact that existence
is not a predicate.

The first step in seeing the plausibility of (D.ii) is to notice
that all phase-sortals are of their very nature *qualifications* or, to
borrow the *Reference and Generality* term, *restrictions* of underlying
more general sortals. *Boy* is definable as *human being that is male
and biologically immature*, and so on. A distinction between substance-sortals and restricted or phase-sortals might be based on
the test whether 'x is no longer f' entails 'x is no-longer' (or, 'for
all f, x is no longer f'). But although this leads one back from
each phase-sortal to a concept of which it is the restriction it
cannot by itself show that the underlying concept which makes
the a which exists at t_i the same something or other as the a
which exists at t_{i+1}, and the underlying concept which makes the
a existing at t_{i+1} the same something as the a which exists at
t_{i+2}, are or restrict one sortal. This remains to be proved.[37]
I know of only one way to prove the stronger principle (D. ii),
or any strong form of D. This proof, so far from resting on the
truth of R, rests on its negation.
We have shown the truth of the weak version of D for phase-
sortals, the truth of (D. i), and the falsity of R. And it is excluded
that a might coincide under a phase sortal f with b, b coincide
under f with c_1, and b coincide under f' with c_2, where f $\neq$ f'
and (g) $(c_1 \underset{g}{\neq} c_2)$. Such a branching situation is picturable in
this way:

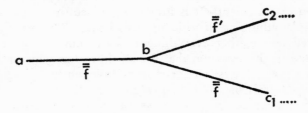

What remains to be disproved is the possibility that a should
coincide with b under f, b with c under f', c under f'' with d ...,
where f, f', f''... are not related by being qualifications of some one
sortal, i.e.:

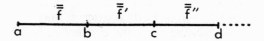

for such f, f′, f″....

Suppose I have found a coincide with b under f and that the individual which is a and b then reaches the end of its f-phase. I have then to decide whether it continues or ceases to exist. Suppose it were said that *any* sortal would do to preserve or continue it in existence provided it applied to whatever was in the place where the individual b was when it ceased to be f. That would be wrong because it would fail to distinguish sufficiently between a thing's being *replaced* and its *continuing to exist*. These are quite different situations in any case, and with Leibniz' Law and the life-histories principle to hand there are even arguments to force us to distinguish them. But in that case there must be some limit on the range of admissible sortals whose applicability would serve to continue a or b, the f thing, in existence. But suppose there were even as many as two such sortals, f′ and g, competing respectively to make b coincide under f′ with c_1 and coincide under g with c_2. Since by the prohibition on branching not both can secure b, why should either?[38] If there is to be any such thing as individuation than there must be some basis on which putative rival claims can be distinguished, and the only basis there could be is this. A thing is legitimately individuated and singled out as one thing through a chain of phases if and only if the chain is so organized that the sortals, f, f′,... describing a thing in adjacent phases, phase f, phase f′, ... are *restrictions of the same sortal*. Now if the relation 'f restricts the same sortal as f″' is an equivalence relation, then this relation will secure that some one underlying sortal extends from any adjacent pair of phases throughout the whole chain back to the beginning and forward to the end of this particular individual's existence. So all that needs to be shown in order to establish (D. ii) is that this relation is indeed an equivalence relation. I will now try to show that it is one.

If f restricts the same sortal as g then g restricts the same sortal as f; f restricts the same sortal as f; so this relation is certainly symmetric and reflexive. Transitivity is more difficult, for it seems that f′ and f″ might both restrict g, and f″ and f‴ both restrict h, without g being the same concept as h. There need be no such thing, it might seem, as one sortal f′ f″ f‴ all restrict.

Suppose that the sortals f′ and f″ restrict a sortal g_1 and that f″ also restricts a sortal h_1. We may fill the situation out a little more by supposing that h_1 is also restricted by a sortal h and that f′ and f″ and g_1 all restrict a sortal g_2 which is an ultimate sortal. (By an ultimate sortal I mean a sortal which either itself restricts no other sortal or else has a sense which both yields necessary and sufficient conditions of persistence for the kind it defines and is such that this sense can be clearly fixed and fully explained without reference to any other sortal which it restricts.)

So far as this description goes it is quite unclear that there need be any sortal of which both g_1 and h_1 are restrictions. The situation would then be one which we can represent diagrammatically in terms of the inclusion relation ⊆ thus

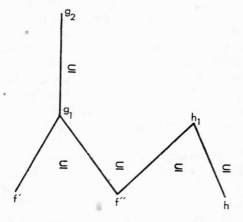

And so far as set theory goes there is nothing impossible about this. There will of course exist the class of $(g_2\text{-or-}h_1)$s $\{\hat{z}(g_2(z)) \lor (h_1(z))\}$, but if this is not a sortal class then it cannot figure in the structure. For, though the structure may be thought of as including all the sortal-concepts whose possibility is implicit in the principles of classification embodied in those sortals actually named and used which belong to the structure, it must contain nothing that is only a sortal by courtesy, such as the dummy sortal *thing* or *space-occupier*.

What is to be shown then, and shown without the unrealistic and absurd prohibitions on cross-classification (diagrammatically speaking, V- and W- shaped substructures) which have disfigured so much of the scant literature on this subject, is that g_1 and h_1 must be restrictions of some common sortal.[39]

To be an f'' is on present suppositions to be a g_1 that is ϕ or an h_1 that is ψ, for some ϕ and ψ or other. Now either the sortals g_1 and h_1 are so related that

$$(x)\,(y)\,\left[((g_1\,(x))\ \&\ (h_1\,(x)))\supset[(x\underset{g_1}{=}y)\equiv(x\underset{h_1}{=}y)]\right]$$

or they are not. If they were not, and if f'' were nevertheless allowed the status of legitimate sortal and were a possible covering concept, then nothing would have been done to exclude the possibility of an object a's being classified as an f'', found to coincide under g_1 with b, and found also to coincide under h_1 with an object c such that $(f)\,(b\underset{f}{\neq}c)$. (A pseudo-sortal of this kind would be *ship or plank-collection*, see pp. 37–8 the discussion of the example from Hobbes which leads to requirement (D. ix).) So if we reject the logical possibility of branching, this option obliges us to reject f'' altogether as a sortal. This does not mean it is not a perfectly legitimate concept but that it is not a concept which can find any place in our structure of sortals. But we had supposed it was a sortal.

Suppose, on the other hand, that g_1 and h_1 are so related that their disjunction yields a covering concept which cannot give rise to branching. Then the cross-classifications which g_1 and h_1 can impose on an object must be subordinate to some logically sound principle of classification under which the object falls. Whether named or unnamed there must then exist a corresponding legitimate sortal which both g_1 and h_1 restrict. In the case of most of the cross-classifications known to me, cases where there really is a point in cross-classification, this sortal will not be very many restriction-steps away; but at worst it will be the ultimate sortal which both g_1 and h_1 restrict.[40] Since 'f_i restricts f_j' is a transitive relation, f' and f'' and h will also restrict whatever sortal g_1 and h_1 restrict. It follows that 'f restricts the same sortal as f" is a transitive relation, which was all that was lacking to show that it was an equivalence-relation. This establishes (D. ii). The stronger form of D follows as trivially as the weaker form followed from (D. i). [For an oversight v. Appx. 5.5].

This proof is impossible without the prohibition on branching and is therefore useless to anybody who will not accept Leibniz' Law. Some adherents of R nevertheless believe the strong form of D. How they would demonstrate it I do not know.

Both demonstrations of D are still rather formal and leave much unexplained. It will be illuminating to go behind them in a less formal manner by saying a little about sufficient conditions of identity.

Leibniz' Law and its contraposition gives a sufficient criterion of difference, but none of identity. The Identity of Indiscernibles yields no sufficient condition. For the strong or classical Identity of Indiscernibles phrased in terms of pure predicates is not a logically true principle.[41] The weak principle of Identity of Indiscernibles, with predicate variable unrestricted and open to predicables with imbedded proper names, is a true principle but does not give us any effective sufficient condition of identity. It is not effective (i) because, for any identity $a=b$, there will be many predicates whose application to one or other of a and b can only be settled by *first* settling whether $a=b$, and (ii) because the weak Identity of Indiscernibles presupposes a prior understanding of the identities of times and places, or of the identities of the particulars whose names turn up inside such predicates as 'five miles S.W. of Big Ben'. In either case we are thrown back onto a prior understanding of the individuation of persisting things.

One way of illuminating the question of sufficient conditions of identity might be (i) to describe a range of favourable causes where continuous observation is possible, and the notion of *spatio-temporal continuity* or *observed coincidence* can be clearly exhibited and imparted, and then (ii) to explain the rationale of the gappy or intermittently observed cases of identity by reference to the theoretical or logical possibility of tracing and observing a persisting thing continuously within the spatio-temporal framework which the less problematic cases would enable us to establish. I have attempted such an account in another place,[42] and all it is necessary to reproduce here is the following truth-condition, T, for an identity-statement '$a=b$'. *If one locates each of the particulars a and b [under covering concept or concepts] and, where appropriate, sc. in the case of 'identity through time', traces a and b through space and time [under covering concepts], one must find that a and b coincide [under some covering concept f].* Now it is in the elucidation of T that we are able to go behind the rather abstract foregoing justification of D and show the quite essential rôle this tautology has to play in all our individuative practices. What particularly needs to be shown is the essential character of the parts of T marked by square brackets.

T is only as clear as it needs to be if we can explain what *coincidence* means or amounts to there. But coincidence in this context is a purely formal notion. There is not, and there could not be, any *general* account of what it is for an arbitrary individual a to coincide or not coincide with an arbitrary individual b; nor could there be any usable account of what it is, in general, to make a mistake or avoid a mistake in tracing a and tracing b to see whether they coincide. To trace a I must know what a *is*. 'Object', 'existent', 'individual', 'part', 'particular', 'substance', 'space-occupier', and kindred dummy-terms, are as useless to say what a is, or what it would be to trace a, as the equally formal notion of *coincidence* is impotent to explain what it would be for unspecified a to coincide with some unspecified b. Now what is needed to specify the sort of object a is is precisely the same kind of thing as what is needed to make the command 'Trace a and trace b and see whether they turn out to coincide with one another' a comprehensible and obeyable command. It is a classification f of a sufficient to settle (adequately for the matter in hand),

(D. iii): what it would be to pick a out or discriminate a (so f must determine a criterion of *identification*),

(D. iv): what it would be to mark a off from other things in a's environment (so f must determine a criterion of *distinctness*—much the same thing as (D. iii)),

(D. v): since a is a persisting thing, what it would be to pick a out again at a later time t within the period of a's existence (so f must determine a criterion of reidentification[43]),

(D. vi): what can and cannot befall a, what changes it can admit, without there ceasing to be any such thing as *a* (again a criterion of reidentification), this being determined either directly (if f is substance-sortal) or indirectly through understanding of something which f restricts (if f is only a phase-sortal).

Nothing less than specification of kinds (D. iii)—(D. vi) is needed to say what *a* is, what it is to trace *a*. But not much more is needed, either, to make it perfectly clear what will have to be found in a particular (favourable) case to settle whether *a* coincides under the concept f with *b*. Knowledge of relevant f, then, is both necessary[44] and sufficient for the simultaneous understanding of what *a* is, of the sense of the question 'is *a* the same as *b*?', and of what establishes or refutes the assertion that *a* is indeed the same as *b*. It follows from all this that we must require of any concept f which is a candidate to answer the question 'same what?' that it should give a principle of tracing which can be *relied upon* to preserve the formal properties of identity, sc. symmetry, transitivity, reflexivity, Leibniz' Law. This is of course a criterion of its being a sortal at all. If it cannot do this we shall not have fixed the sense of the identity-statements it covers to be the sense of *identity*-statements. (See also below p. 43.)

If this is right then it opens a route already mentioned to the notion of *a material substance*. For it seems that we are in a position to use freely such *a priori* knowledge as we have of the notion of identity, viz. its formal properties, to work out the formal requirements which any f will have to satisfy in order to count as competent to elucidate the coincidence or identity conditions for a given kind of individual. Coincidence under f will have to be genuinely sufficient to secure the satisfaction of these *a priori* formal requirements. Otherwise f cannot adequately gloss identity-questions of the form 'is *x* the same... as *y*?'—they wouldn't have the answer-conditions of *identity*-questions.

In this way, although we despair of an external characterisation, we can build up the notion of a sortal, and so of a substance, as it were from the inside. We characterize it purely formally. (D. i)—(D. vi) are already of course part of such a characterization, as are D itself and the negation of R. I shall rapidly draw attention to a few more of the formally determined conditions on any concept's being a substance-concept and indicate how such a formal account of substance would be extended.

(D. vii): If f is a substance-concept for *a*, then *a* is f throughout the time in which there is such a thing as *a*; and (because f or some equivalent sortal gives the sense of *a*'s proper name) the proposition that *a* is not f is self-contradictory.

(D. viii): If f is a substance concept for *a*, and g is a sortal (but not necessarily a substance-concept) applicable to *a*, then, if $a =_f b$, *b* is, was, or will be a g and is, was, or will be the same g as *a* is.

We have already used the negation of R and the formal prohibition on branching in the demonstration of (D. ii). But a little more needs to be said about the cases where competition seems to arise between individuals which both have a claim to coincide with something. Hobbes puts this problem forcibly against those who regard 'unity of form' as a *principium individu-ationis*

'two bodies existing both at once would be one and the same numerical body. For if, for example, that ship of Theseus, concerning the difference whereof made by continued reparation in taking out the old planks and putting in new, the sophisters of Athens were wont to dispute, were, after all the planks were changed, the same numerical ship it was at the beginning; and if some man had kept the old planks as they were taken out, and by putting them afterwards together in the same order, had again made a ship of them, this, without doubt, had also been the same numerical ship with that which was at the beginning; and so there would have been two ships numerically the same, which is absurd.'[45]

Our version of the unity of form view makes coincidence under the concept *ship* a sufficient condition but it escapes this difficulty because it decisively favours the repaired ship.[46] That ship's persistence and spatio-temporal continuity with Theseus' ship make it the dominant claimant. This simply follows from what was meant by *coincidence*. To secure this, however, coincidence must be coincidence under an f which determines when a claimant is good enough.[47] For Hobbes' case the sortal *ship* does do this. More difficult cases are conceivable, however. Notoriously there is the case where an amoeba divides exactly in half and becomes two amoebas. We are committed to say about this

D

that, since not both can be identical with the original amoeba, and since neither amoeba has a better claim than the other amoeba, neither of them can be identical with it.[48] ('Becomes' must then receive an analysis making it correspond to ordinary 'becomes' as constitutive 'is' corresponds to the ordinary 'is' of identity. The matter of the original amoeba—the 'it'—is the 'fusion', or the matter, of the two new ones taken together). But if coincidence under f is to be *genuinely* sufficient we must not withhold identity in this case simply because transitivity is threatened. There must be something *independently* wrong. And of course there is. The original amoeba does not in fact pass into either of the competing amoebas in the required way, and there is a breach in what we ought in any case to require by way of continuity. (Imagine the process with one of the later amoebas becoming invisible; exactly half of the original amoeba—neither a more nor a less important portion—seeming to vanish. This would not be satisfactory as a piece of coinciding.) It is of course impossible to say *in general* what is required for adequate coincidence. But a requirement which can be made determinate enough for given choice of f is this schema:

(D. ix): If f is a substance concept for *a* then *coincidence under* f must be a determinate notion, clear and decisive enough to exclude this situation: *a* is traced under f and counts as coinciding with *b* under f, and *a* is traced under f and counts as coinciding with *c* under f while nevertheless *b* does not coincide under f with *c*.

(D. x): The falsity of R seems to exclude those essentially disjunctive substance-concepts, (f *or* g), coincidence under which, as remarked in proving (D. ii), might allow *a* to be the same (f *or* g) as *b*, and the same (f *or* g) as a *c* which was distinct under every covering concept from *b*.[49] Some disjunctive sortals are quite innocuous in this respect e.g. when the f is subordinate to the g, or when the f and the g are both subordinate to a higher sortal. (For example *animal or mouse* is innocuous—*a* cannot be the same mouse as but a different animal from *b*—and this complex sortal reduces simply to *animal*). They will not be innocuous in this respect unless the corresponding conjunctive sortal is a logically satisfiable concept (e.g. *animal and mouse*, which reduces in the opposite direction to *mouse*). Disjunctive sortals of this kind seem however to be as superfluous as they are innocuous.

(D. xi): If f is a substance-concept for *a* then however indefinitely and unforeseeably the chain of a's coincidents *a*, *a'*, *a''*, *a'''* … extends, then whatever is truly or falsely *applicable* to a member of the chain must be truly or falsely *applicable* to every member of the chain whatever. But then all f's must belong to one *category*. (*A fortiori* from Leibniz' Law, and trivial, but relevant to some allegedly logically possible metamorphoses, e.g. that of Proteus into *fire* at Odyssey IV, 453–463.)

It will conclude the discussion of D, and show why the distinct claim, C, of Part One, 1.1, was wrong or only an approximate truth, if we ask whether we can add

(D. xii): If f is a substance-concept, then there must exist the possibility of a definite and finite answer to the question 'how many fs are there in region r at time t?'

Though most substance-concepts in my usage do satisfy this condition (as do most sortals), and though something like (Dxii) is often used as a *criterion* of being a sortal, both (Dii) and C are in their full generality false. It is a sufficient condition of being a sortal, because, given that a man knows the natural numbers and uses them correctly on a given occasion, then to see if he answers the question 'how many fs?' correctly is to see whether he locates fs and isolates them correctly from their background and from one another. But it is not, I think, a necessary condition of being an acceptable covering concept. It is possible to conceive of circumstances under which it would be a perfectly clear question whether you at t_1 saw, (e.g.) *the same oily wave as I* saw at t_1, although there was not a definite way of *counting* the waves or the oily waves in the area of sea we were observing. There might be acute difficulties of decision (not merely practical difficulties surmountable with photographs, etc.) involved in the general enterprise of trying to count the waves. These difficulties might simply not exist for one or two specific waves. For the decision may automatically have been made, and the question of the extent of the wave or waves simply settled, by the manner of reference to this wave or these waves used in the specific question about the wave I saw and the wave you saw. (This is not to say it will always have been satisfactorily settled. If there is not a complete overlap of extent, for example, then the transitivity of identity may be threatened.)

Again, coincidence under the concept *crown* gives a perfectly satisfactory way of answering identity-questions for crowns. But there is no definite way of counting crowns. The Pope's crown is made of crowns. There is no definite answer, when the Pope is wearing his crown, to the question 'how many crowns does he have on his head?' But is *crown* not a substance-concept? (Compare *cell* and *crystal* and, substance apart, note items in other categories such as colours and their shades, quantities, etc.). [See now Appendix 5.2].

PART THREE

3.1. *Summary of conclusions of first two parts.*

(1) The formal properties of identity include transitivity, reflexivity, symmetry, and Leibniz' Law. Regardless of whether the meaning of the notion be completely exhaustible by these formal principles, *at least* these principles are integral to the purport of '=' and '='.
     f

(2) If (1) above is true, then R is false.

(3) There are two distinct standpoints from which D and the covering-concept requirement can be maintained. It may be held that *a* could be the same f as *b* without being the same g. Or it may be held that to say what *a* is is automatically to provide an f which determines the truth-grounds of '*a=b*'. It is only the second defence of D which is correct.

(4) To see what guarantees there must be against a case of R, and against other violations of the logical properties of identity, is to see how the notion of a substance can be given the beginnings of a purely formal characterisation.

3.2. *Essentialist postscript to the first two parts.*

From perfectly extensional principles, Leibniz' Law in particular, we have reached what might pejoratively be described as a *viciously essentialist* view of individuation. It is certainly an intemperately anti-conventionalist view. This should perhaps be surprising, or should surprise those who find the whole supposed contrast between something called nominalism and something called essentialism an intelligible contrast. It should also surprise those who mechanically suppose that extensionalism has necessarily to 'side with' nominalism at every point on every issue (whatever these worn out old labels signify). But, apart from one relatively clear and here irrelevant issue about teleological explanation, it seems to me that the whole conflict between the two positions is usually explained in terms of such incredible vagueness that it is quite obscure what counts as a rebuttal of the charge of essentialism. All I can do here to rebut it is simply to remark:

(i) That anyone who objects to these conclusions on nominalist grounds must also say what is wrong with the way they are arrived at. So far as I can tell the starting point is thoroughly extensional and should be perfectly acceptable to a nominalist.

(ii) That although my conclusions (e.g. (Dvii)) reinstate some *de re* modalities of the form $\square$ (fa), where f is a substance sortal, they do nothing to suggest that the correct way of generalizing such is the mysterious $\square$ [($\exists x$) (f(x))]—which would presumably have the consequence that this was ontologically the poorest of all possible worlds—rather than ($\exists x$)($\square$f(x)).

(iii) That if there is anything clear about the supposed contrast between *discovering* and *inventing* a concept (and if the nature of the contrast is not intended to have the absurd consequence that before we possessed the concept f there were no fs), then nothing which is said here determines which is the right view of our arrival at concepts. It is an equal duty on both sides to explain how the fact that there are empirical as well as logical constraints on the admissibility of a sortal does not (if it does not) count in favour of the discovery view. On both views, again, it can and always must be an empirical question whether one has in front of one what really is an f.

(iv) My essentialism simply derives from a willingness to pay more than lip service to the idea that we cannot single out bare space-occupying matter. And it goes on to take seriously the consequence of this, namely that how we do our singling out determines both *what* we single out, and (which is the same thing) the *principle of individuation* of what we single out, and (again the same thing) the *conditions of the existence* of what we have singled out. Its existence is independent of our thought (cp. Hobbes' definition[50]—*a body is that, which having no dependence upon our thought, is coincident or coextended with some part of space*), even if our individuation of it (obviously) cannot be. It was there before we picked it out—its *modus essendi* is prior to its *modus intelligendi*, if you like,—but to pick it out you have to pick *it* out. What else would you expect? If you want this tautology dressed up then you may say that our only access to its *modus essendi* is via its *modus intelligendi*. There is no point in this Byzantine word-ritual and its terminological apparatus. But once the tautology is dressed up in this way, do not complain about *what* is dressed up. Complain about the vestments, which are as unnecessary as they are threadbare.

PART FOUR

4.1. *Self, Body and Spatio-Temporal Continuity*

The so-called memory-criterion of personal identity is often contrasted with the criterion of the spatio-temporal continuity of a living body. At the moment I think the spatio-temporal criterion is widely supposed to be (i) a perfectly clear criterion of personal identity, (ii) a criterion which might very easily clash with the memory-criterion, and (iii) a criterion which is generally or always to be preferred to the memory criterion. This is not universally supposed and the memory-criterion still has its advocates. I shall show in due course why that is not surprising. But memory theorists do not differ from bodily theorists in thinking in terms of possible clashes of memory and bodily criteria. In this Part I shall argue that a criterion of bodily continuity is not the only or the best kind of spatio-temporal criterion for persons—another is available—, and that no correct spatio-temporal criterion of personal identity can conflict with any correct memory-criterion or character-continuity criterion of personal identity. It is this which prevents the notion of person from falling in two. (By a criterion of identity for fs I mean something logically *constitutive* of the identity of fs, and potentially analytical of what it is to be an f. A criterion C only qualifies as the criterion for " $=$ " if the satisfaction of C *logically implies* the
$_{f}$
satisfaction of a transitive, symmetrical reflexive relation; even though the empirical *tests* for the satisfaction of C need only preserve *de facto* this equivalence property of " $=$ ". Compare
$_{f}$
my nationality, criterially determined by the place of my birth or other considerations, with one test of it, *the passport I carry*.)

Some philosophers concede so much to the idea of a clash of criteria that they even maintain that we have two quite different, equally good, and potentially contradictory sufficient conditions of personal identity which co-exist uneasily under the terms of a precarious armistice. For these philosophers it is as if Frege and Leśnieskwi had never lived or written a word on the subject of soundness of concepts.[51] They apparently feel extreme optimism about the possibility of simply 'reading off' the logical properties of a concept and reporting what they see; and in this case simple inspection apparently tells them (a) that *person* is a unitary concept, (b) that it has diverse and quite contingently related criteria. It is not explained how this would differ from 'just seeing' that 'person' was an ambiguous or even defective concept. Nor is there any attempt, at very worst, to devise a sound, even though complex and unhomogeneous, sufficient condition of being the same person. But I hope to show that even such an extraordinary view as this has sources which will repay study and which we can use the results of previous Parts to illuminate.

I shall approach the matter from the direction of what is thought of as 'the other' criterion, supposedly the most hard-minded option, the requirement of bodily continuity. This necessitates a rapid preliminary traverse of some well-trodden ground.

Upholders of the bodily criterion may characteristically arrive at their view of personal identity by a number of routes. Some are impressed by the point that for me to remember falling over is for me to remember *my* falling over. 'To remember an experience entails claiming it as an experience of one's own; from which it would seem to follow that personal identity cannot be founded on this type of memory since it is already presupposed by it.'[52] Ayer goes on to say that this circle 'may be only apparent', but the point he makes is aptly reinforced by Williams' argument that the whole distinction between a true and an apparent memory of the experience of falling over is at once crucial to the application of the concept of remembering X-ing and radically dependent on some 'other' criterion than memory to anchor the memory-criterion and to decide the question whether the fall I claim to remember ever actually happened to me at all. Other philosophers may be equally impressed by another argument of Williams' that no memory claim criterion can be genuinely sufficient, however rich and complex its requirements, because it would sometimes have both to allow and to accord equal weight to the pretensions of two non-identical memory-claimants.

These arguments apparently lead to the conclusion that the criterion of individuation for A is the same criterion as the criterion of individuation for A's body. Yet this conclusion is itself full of difficulties. To begin with, my body lasts longer than I do. Or perhaps I last longer than it. Certainly we don't last the same amount of time. How then can we be the same? Second, the proposed criterion now seems to ride intolerably roughshod over the memory criterion. If memory is as irrelevant as it now seems to be, how did it ever get into the discussion at all? Thirdly, there is the feeling that my identity cannot possibly be the identity of a body I can clearly imagine myself exchanging for another body, or even imagine myself losing altogether. This feeling has recently been eloquently expressed and subtly diagnosed by Thomas Nagel,[53] but it is of respectable antiquity and was voiced by Thomas Reid, 'The identity . . . which we ascribe to bodies, whether natural or artificial, is not perfect identity; it is rather something which, for convenience of speech, we call identity' . . . 'Questions about the identity of a body are often questions about words'. But for persons, Reid says, 'Identity has no ambiguity and admits not of degrees . . . the notion of it is precise'.[54] People as we know them are irreducibly spatio-temporal. They are in places at times. They take room. If they are spatio-temporal objects, then surely their principle of individuation must be spatio-temporal. And yet, if these difficulties are genuine, how can their identity-criterion be spatio-temporal?

To see the answer to this problem, and make the appropriate concessions to these three objections, is to see the essential unity of the concept of a person and the equivalence of the revised spatio-temporal criterion to any admissible memory criterion of personal identity. This equivalence does not arise simply and trivially from the role of the spatio-temporal criterion in determining the veridicality of single claims to remember X-ing or Y-ing. The spatio-temporal criterion and the memory criterion, when it is properly founded in the notion of cause, inform and regulate one another *reciprocally*—indeed they are really aspects of a single criterion. For the requirement of spatio-temporal continuity is quite empty until we say continuity *under what concept* (see Part Two). And it will be argued that we cannot specify the right concept without mention of the behaviour, characteristic functioning, and capacities of a person, including the capacity to remember some sufficient amount of his past.[55] It is this characteristic functioning which gives the relevant kind of spatio-temporal continuity for the kinds of parcel of matter we individuate when we individuate persons.

4.2.   The first difficulty in the straight bodily criterion, that my body lasts longer than I do, is reminiscent of a formally comparable difficulty which attaches to Aristotle's definition of the soul:

'Inevitably then the soul [*psūchē*] is the substance [*ousia*], substance in the sense of being the form [*eidos*], of a body which is the right kind of body in nature to be a living body. But substance in this sense is actuality [*entelecheia* ⁓ *realization in matter*]—the actuality then of a body of a certain sort. There are two senses of actuality, one analogous to the possession of knowledge, the other analogous to the exercise of knowledge. Obviously the sort of actuality we mean here is of the former kind, that which is analogous to possession of knowledge. Both sleep and waking depend on the presence of soul. The former is analogous to mere possession of knowledge the latter analogous to the exercise of knowledge. And possession of knowledge is what comes first in any man. So soul is the first actuality [analogous to possession of knowledge] of a living or potentially living natural body.' (*De Anima* 412[a]19-27).

Aristotle goes on to say that the body must have organs and that the form or actuality must be the form or actuality of a living body possessed of these. Later in the book this requirement is explained and amplified, and any semblance of circularity attaching to the notion of *life* and *living* is removed, by a careful disassembly of the notion of *psūchē* and life into a nested series of higher and higher faculties, sensation, imagination, memory, reason and so forth.

Aristotle's terminology is perhaps unfamiliar or uninviting enough to make it worth while, before I go into all the difficulties, to suggest the great interest of Aristotle's doctrine and to make out its relevance to the problem of personal identity.

Psūchē is conventionally rendered *soul*, an English word whose difficulties match all the difficulties of the Greek word. (That is to say that it is not quite clear what Aristotle's definition of *psūchē* is a definition of.) But for our purposes it will not do

very much harm to think of *psūchē* as much the same notion as
person. Aristotle does not scruple to say that the soul is sad, is
delighted, is brave, is afraid, grows angry; and it is certain that
the identity of my *psūchē* cannot diverge from the identity of me.
So even if Aristotle sometimes insists that we are sad, delighted,
etc. and alive, *by the psūchē which we have* (408[b3] following) his
definition of soul, and its implications for identity of soul, carry
over virtually immediately to persons and the identity of these.
The beauty of his account is that it makes it impossible to develop
an account of what a living body is in isolation from an account
of what sentient functions and characteristically human functions
are.[56]   Indeed by Aristotle's method it is logically impossible to
end up in the extraordinary position of the dual criterion theorist
who cannot explain what makes *person* a unitary concept. Aristotle
can claim

> 'So there is no call to ask whether the soul and the body are
> one, just as there is no call to ask this question with the wax
> and the impression in the wax, nor any call to ask this
> question for any substance and the matter of which this
> substance is composed. Although "is" and "one" have
> many different uses the canonical use of "one" is to count
> materially realized actual substances.' (412[b6]).

This is something like the position in which I think we want
to end up. For things and their matter see again the discussion of
examples (α) and (β) in 1.4. But the difficulty is this. If we wish
to state the doctrine that matter is to form as body is to soul, and
to take this idea seriously, then we must have a way of saying
what matter is the matter in which the soul is realized. This is a
problem which Aristotle takes as seriously as his detractors. Now
this specification is fairly easy to achieve for the merely illustrative
example which Aristotle introduces a little later in the discussion,
the matter of which an axe is made and the axe. The axe is an
artifact whose actuality is defined by the requirement that it
should be capable of cutting in a certain way and it is realized in
(or made out) of that matter. The matter is iron. But when we
come to a particular animal or human the situation is slightly
different. Of course we can specify the matter as 'this flesh and
bones'. But in this case there is competition for possession of the
matter. For 'human body' is a perfectly good sortal or substance-

word, and unfortunately it is *already* in occupation of this flesh
and bones. And the principle of individuation for *human body* is
not quite the same as that for a *person*. A blunted axe is still an
axe, and a decomposing human body is still a human body. Yet
if *psūchē* is the *ousia*, f, of *x* then it would seem that *x* must *be* an f.
(If f is the account of what *x* is then it would seem that *x* must
satisfy the sortal predicate f.) But then the living body *is* a soul.
If a natural living body is a certain complex of matter and form
then surely that form is the form of that natural living body. And
that form is *psūchē* or *person*. It is then difficult that Aristotle
gives us no other way of reading *living body* (*sōma metechon*
zōēs) than *body which is alive*. And we have not been told how to
parse this any differently from *man who is white*. But to be a man
who is white is not to go on resisting sunburn on pain of extinc-
tion. One survives, the same man but not the same colour.[57]
Why should it be any different with a living body which then
becomes a dead body. Why isn't it still a psūchē?[58]

I think it is clear that what we have done here is in effect to
rediscover the 'is' of constitution (see 1.4). The only logically
hygienic way of sorting out Aristotle's analogy:

matter: form : : [living] body: soul

is to explain that if one refers to the matter *m* by a reference made
as to a stuff then the relation between the form-sortal f and *m*
will be that the f is *constitutively* the *m*, or alternatively that the f is
(predicatively) the thing of which *m* is the matter. This is not
quite all that needs explaining, however. What we have explained
so far is the possibility of taking the analogy as equivalent to:

matter : form : : flesh & bones : person.

Two questions are still outstanding. The first is the competition
between body and *psūchē* or person. For surely we can equally
well say:

matter : form : : flesh & bones : living body.

And then we have two things, a person and a human body,
occupying (or being embodied or realized in) the same matter,
and normally occupying it concurrently for the period of the life of
the person. We then have two non-identical things in the same
place at the same time. But this is not really a problem, because it
will be found that room was carefully left for this in our reformu-
lation of the principle that two things cannot be in the same place

at the same time. We stipulated: two things *of the same kind*.[59] And
if an uncontroversial example is needed, then it is provided by
(γ) of 1.4, Cleopatra's Needle, the landmark-cum-monument, and
the stone which is at once an individual in its own right and
constitutive of that monument.

The second question which is outstanding is the formulation
of the principle of individuation for the second claimant on the
flesh and bones, the person who is strictly speaking non-identical
with the living body. As Aristotle himself is the first to insist,
you cannot simply define a new kind of entity into existence,
white-man or living-body (contrasted with man who is white and
body which is alive respectively). It takes more than a simple
decree.[57] You would have at very least to explain what the
principle of individuation was for this new entity which was to be
non-identical with the body and yet so closely associated with it,
sharing its matter but not its persistence conditions. This brings
me to the original second objection to the criterion of bodily
continuity, its cavalier and slipshod treatment of all other criteria
such as character-continuity and sufficient or potentially sufficient
experience-memory.

4.3. What interests memory-theorists and what bodily-
theorists ignore is something which is surely both central to the
notion of a person and utterly distinctive of it; it is also something for which Aristotle could readily have found a place in his
hierarchy of the functions conceptually constitutive of human
life: an individual's memory of some sufficient number of the
things which have happened to him *as* things which have happened to him. To be a person (in any unattenuated sense of the
word) is to be capable of believing and ceasing to believe things
on evidence, which in its turn requires the possibility of memory of
experience. One can be forgetful and enjoy the status of person.
But one must have the biological potentiality of experience-
memory of a sufficiently sophisticated sort.

Our problem is not so much to demonstrate the importance
of these Lockean contentions as to improve on existing accounts
of the relation of this conceptual feature of persons to the other,
apparently hard-headed, conceptual requirements of their bodily
continuity.

Sydney Shoemaker has proposed the following thought-experiment.[60]

'Suppose that medical science has developed a technique whereby a surgeon can completely remove a person's brain from his head, examine or operate on it, and then put it back in his skull (regrafting the nerves, blood-vessels, and so forth) without causing death or permanent injury. . . . One day a surgeon discovers that an assistant has made a horrible mistake. Two men, a Mr. Brown and a Mr. Robinson, had been operated on for brain tumors, and brain extractions had been performed on both of them. At the end of the operations, however, the assistant inadvertently put Brown's brain in Robinson's head, and Robinson's brain in Brown's head. One of these men immediately dies, but the other, the one with Robinson's body and Brown's brain, eventually regains consciousness. Let us call the latter 'Brownson'. . . . He recognizes Brown's wife and family (whom Robinson had never met), and is able to describe in detail events in Brown's life, always describing them as events in his own life. Of Robinson's past life he evidences no knowledge at all. Over a period of time he is observed to display all of the personality traits, mannerisms, interests, likes and dislikes, and so on that had previously characterized Brown, and to act and talk in ways completely alien to the old Robinson.
'What would we say if such a thing happened? There is little question that many of us would be inclined, and rather strongly inclined, to say that while Brownson has Robinson's body he is actually Brown. But if we did say this we certainly would not be using bodily identity as our criterion of personal identity. To be sure, we are supposing Brownson to have *part* of Brown's body, namely his brain. But it would be absurd to suggest that brain identity is our criterion of personal identity.'

I think the Aristotelian view of what a life and a *psūchē* are, taken in conjunction with a causal theory of memory and our previous analysis of spatio-temporal continuity, put us in a position to improve a bit on Shoemaker's rather hasty conclusion. Abandoning Aristotle's terminology, the point is that spatio-temporal continuity under the concept *psūchē* or *person* (living-body as opposed to living body) is not quite the same as spatio-temporal continuity under the concept *body*. And if we take the conceptual analysis of vital functions as seriously as Aristotle and the memory theorist do, and as seriously as anyone who thought Brownson was the same man as Brown would have to take it, then surely what matters is not bodily continuity but the continuity of Brown's life and vital functions as they are planted in one body and recognizably and traceably transposed in another body. But Brown's life and vital functions define an individual in the category of substance. They define a person. The problem then is to describe a coherent continuity principle for this kind of individual, one which will satisfy the formal conditions of substancehood sketched in Part Two.

The kind of individual we are to define is not made of anything other than flesh and bones, but, unlike the body with which it at some times shares its matter it has a characterization in functional terms which confer the rôle, as it were, of *individuating nucleus* on a particular brain which is the seat of a particular set of memory-capacities. The brain does not figure in the *a priori* account of *person* or *same person* except perhaps under the description 'seat of memory and other functionally characteristic capacities'. But *de facto* it plays this rôle of individuating nucleus. For the brain happens as a matter of scientific fact to be the bodily part which plays the rôle whose importance the memory theory and the Aristotelian theory of vital functions can establish on a purely conceptual basis. Oddly enough Aristotle foresaw or almost foresaw both Shoemaker's thought-experiment and our answer to the problem which it poses.[61] (Although Aristotle cast the heart for the rôle in question, he even foresaw that the functions which he ascribed to the heart might really belong to the brain.)

It would be a long task to revise Aristotle's conceptual analysis of the hierarchy of vital functions and to verify in detail that the formally necessary conditions of substance-hood sketched in Part Two were satisfied by a principle of individuation for persons which permitted their individuative nucleus to be the brain or the core of the central nervous system. It will be suggestive enough of a complete theory to try to verify the satisfaction of one of the most troublesome conditions, (D. ix) of Part Two. (See Page 38). If we individuate people by tracing functionally essential cerebral or neural material then what guarantee can we have that principle (D. ix) will not be violated?

Irritatingly enough the amoeba problem repeats itself. It so happens that mammalian brains are roughly symmetrical and

> 'the two halves can be entirely separated to a great depth with only minimal disturbance of normal function.'[62]

It is true that in the case of a man's brain the two halves of it are not equal in status and that if a surgeon separated them one half would be clever and the other half moronic, but nevertheless at least one way in which one might have to look at this is to suppose that

> 'the surgeon's knife has turned [the brain] into two independent brains and two independent consciousnesses. Both of these new brains would, presumably, remember having been the single brain which was there before. One would remember this with satisfaction, at least providing it was cured from the mental disorder the whole brain had had. The other would regret its present stupidity and wish it still had abilities now irrevocably lost.'[62]

The evident intelligibility of J. S. Griffith's view of the matter, when taken in conjunction with the transitivity of identity and aggravated by the clear logical possibility of the permanent transplantation of brains, poses a grave problem—grave anyway if we are not to be engulfed by the hordes who would have us say that 'we can say what we like' here, or that we shall simply have to 'fix things up', or that this matter is a mere 'matter for decision' (which I take to mean arbitrary decision). No doubt it is in some far fetched and fantastic sense of the words a 'matter for decision' whether to talk of *people*. But once we do so and this 'convention' exists, there are complicated and potentially unobvious logical and conceptual constraints on the concepts *person* and *same person* which we shall have to observe on pain of speaking inconsistently, and therefore not truly, or even nonsensically. To offer to 'fix things up' is to suggest that all considerations germane to the point or interest of the concept *person* have already been dealt with, that the force of the existing convention is already exhausted. This may sometimes (rather rarely) be so, but one has to show it separately for each particular case.

Problems like the present one about personal identity are

PART FOUR § 4.3 53

often referred to—'what we or lawyers or judges would say if the problem actually arose'. But although it is true that such people as judges would bear in mind the normal interest of applying the substantive *person* we want to reserve the right (a) to criticise what they say and (b) to determine whether the decision does what such decisions do not standardly do, changes the concept, or changes the use of the concept. And we want to be able to say how exactly it changes either of these things (which, as will appear, are different things). If what they decide in some peculiar case has the effect of making Brown into a peculiar sort of universal—a particular social rôle for any qualitatively suitable actor—then we want to have reserved the right to try to show this. Lawyers and judges are not authorities on the differences between particular and universal or identity of individuals and similarity of individuals.

Suppose that we split Brown's brain and house the two halves in two different bodies. The difficulty is that there is no inclination at all to suppose here that our 'decision' floats free of the interests which normally animate our application of the concept *person*. Since there is memory character and life in both brain transplants it precisely cannot. And if there is the slightest inclination to suppose that the inferiority of one of the brain transplants counts for anything, then it is scarcely an effort of the imagination to change this feature of the thought-experiment.

We are supposing that the transplanted persons, Brown I and Brown II, claim to remember exactly the same things, that they are equally intelligent, and that they are equally at home in their new bodies. In this case, where cerebral material is actually transplanted we cannot simply disregard their (claimed) memories. For we understand far too well *why* they have these memories. On the other hand if we say each is the same person as Brown, we shall have to say Brown I is the same person as Brown II. That is an inescapable part of what was meant by saying that each was the same person as Brown. But Brown I will have all sorts of experiences which Brown II will not. They will be in different places and have separate experiences from now on. And they will communicate *interpersonally*.

The most fundamental form of our difficulty is this. The bodily coincidence criterion of personal identity satisfied condition

E

(D. ix), but it left the functional and memory criteria wholly unexplained and at some points it gave the wrong criterion of identity for persons. We undertook to define another concept to be the concept *person*, using a criterion of functionally relevant bodily material. This proved inadequate to generate a genuinely sortal concept because it could not define anything which could strictly qualify to belong to the category of substance. And persons are substances. The difficulty is unsurprising because 'claims to remember X-ing on such and such an occasion' is a multiply satisfiable predicate and 'is causally essential to the performance of such and such functions' applies as well to stuffs as it does to things. Neither singly nor jointly could they guarantee coincidence as a one-one relation. And *in a way* the difficulty is unworrying. The thought-experiment with brain splitting forces us to conceive of circumstances in which we should have to think of consciousness or personhood as something which could belong derivatively in the category of stuff, and it forces us to conceive that this stuff could be done up in separate parcels which could have additional separate histories of their own for such time as they were separate parcels, as well as having other bits of shared history. We should then individuate persons like the members of clones.[63] This thought-experiment does not even force us to think of an entirely new sense of 'person' (though we should have to say a little about 'remember'). Sortal concepts perfectly standardly enjoy the option of entering the category of stuff for as long as they wish. (Cleopatra's Needle is made of a stone; and (ghoulishly) Tantalus offered Demeter some Pelops. She took Pelops' shoulder, which was subsequently made good in ivory. It surely does not much matter for present purposes whether we say here that good sortals like *stone* or Pelops [*man*] have an autonomous use in the category of stuff or prefer to say they have a special use in their own category to force the reinterpretation of 'made of x' = 'made of the stuff which makes up x', and 'some of x' = 'some of the stuff making up x'.) The principal importance of the thought-experiment is to make us reflect on what is logically required to operate *person* and *same person* not like *same clone* but straightforwardly in the category of substance, if necessary by analogy with *same cutting*. We can describe in a coherent and perfectly adequate way what it would be to need both uses of the phrase 'same person'. It would no more threaten Leibniz' Law than the existence of clones and amoebas threatens it. But our present question is what is involved in operating it in the category of substance. Let us ignore further problems about clone-persons. [See now Appx. 5.7]

(D. ix) would be satisfied by our reverting to the whole human body for our coincidence condition . But that is not the only course open to us. What (D. ix) requires of any substance sortal f is only that *coincidence under f* should exclude the possibility of splitting. If coincidence under the concept *person* were made *logically equivalent* to brain-coincidence this condition would still go unsatisfied. It is not *logically* excluded that people should remember with their feet or their fingers, or that the conceptually essential functions should be distributed to several different parts of the body. It would be better, after a conceptual analysis of the essential and characteristic vital functions, to analyse *person* in such a way that coincidence under the concept *person* logically required the *continuance in one organized parcel of all that was causally sufficient and causally necessary to the continuance of essential and characteristic functioning, no autonomously sufficient part achieving autonomous and functionally separate existence*. This logically excludes splitting, and makes the right empirical question arise at the right place. 'Have we *in this case* transferred all that was causally sufficient and necessary?', which involves both general questions and particular questions of causality.

If we proceeded like this two questions would remain. The first would be whether, if both halves of the brain were equipollent, it would be enough to secure identity of person to destroy one half of the brain and transplant the other. It must be admitted that this proposal would be very much more satisfactory in a number of ways than anything one could achieve by adjustments of the memory claim criterion criticised by Williams.[47] The present proposal would leave more room for the causality which is conceptually involved in memory, and it would provide a better underwriting of identity as an equivalence relation than any putative laws of unique disembodied psychical transfer, which would have to handle uncomfortably indefinite tracts of time and space. It is better than that, but although there may be more room here than usual for manoeuvre I think that, strictly speaking, the proposal is inadequate and that we must resort to the degenerate 'clone' use of *person* to describe the case, even if uniqueness is guaranteed. For one of the constraints which should act on us here is the likeness of what happens to the surviving half in this case to what happens to it in the unallowable double transplant case. And surely we do not want to say that we cannot tell whether or not we have proper coincidence and genuine identity in a case where we are uncertain about the fate of one half! I am not sure, even here, that we have really reached a pure case for (arbitrary) decision.

The other outstanding question about our coincidence requirement is its operation in a world more or less like ours in which one half of the brain is in fact much better than the other. 'Essential and characteristic functioning' is vague. It has to be vague to let vague questions remain vague questions. The answer to the question depends on how bad the inferior half is. If it were sufficiently moronic I imagine we could call it the person's shadow or *umbra* and accord the favoured half full identity with the originating person, while describing the relation between *umbra* and parent brain on the pattern of what we should say about the relation between tree and cutting. But if the inferior half were not moronic I think we should have to operate the member-of-a-clone concept for each half. We have here to make up our mind about something which involves a question of degree but *pace* Thomas Reid this imports nothing of degree into any assertion of identity which we may end up with. Nor would such questions be arbitrary or a matter of words if they arose in any concrete case. They could be arbitrary only if they arose exactly on the narrow frontier lying between highly motivated decisions in the making of which we were not free at all.

4.4.   This concludes the discussion arising out of our original second objection, and it suggests the answer to the third, the objection that any spatio-temporal criterion makes my identity too arbitrary or too merely verbal a subject-matter. The previous three Parts of this monograph have suggested that there is nothing verbal or arbitrary even about the identity of ordinary material objects. A covering concept f serves to make an identity-question determinate, and this concept f arises out of the very act of reference to the items mentioned in the identity-question itself. Of course we need not refer to or ask questions about fs, and we may account for and exhaust the matter of the world by dividing it into gs instead. But then identity questions about gs will have in their turn to be determinate.

It is common to feel a difference between *person* and other sortals and to construe this as a difference between non-material and material substances.[54] But the difference we feel has to do with us, not with these sortals. We *are* persons and while we recognize this and raise questions about the *identity of persons* we cannot opt out of the use of the sortal *person*. That is the relevant covering-concept for the questions we ask. The sole peculiarity of *person* is that it is more than usually odd to call it a 'decision' of ours to employ this sortal. But this peculiarity belongs only with us, and it leads to no distinction between the concept *person* and other sortal-concepts in respect of determinateness, or absoluteness. The preceding discussion, in which we tried to devise a coincidence-condition for *person* showed that (*pace* Hume, Reid, Descartes) the concept *person* can be as troublesome or vague for identity-questions as any other concept can. It was also shown there how and why all spatio-temporal criteria will systematically follow and accord with any admissible subjective criteria beloved of Cartesians. When we see why exactly this is we also see that it can have no tendency whatever to prove that we are more than flesh and bones (in the constitutive sense of 'are').

But there is one thing which I think the unitary functional criterion does bring out. If physicalism is meant to be the denial of the primitiveness of the concept of person then physicalism is false, though quite unexcitingly false. We are not identical with our bodies. Our bodies don't know arithmetic or play games. We can understand this now for the truism it is. And the demonstration of how the functional criterion can carry us from one body to another while we are nevertheless material entities in space and in time provides a suitably restrained vindication of Strawson's similar claim in his book *Individuals*. The concept which belongs to physiological science is *human organism*, *human body*, or whatever. We can imagine such things being replenished with spare hands, spare kidneys *and with spare brains*. The repair need not preserve character-continuity or memory-continuity. But if this is the physicalistic way of looking at the individuation of *persons* then the way of physicalism is wrong. Irreducibly psychological concepts are required to define an entity with the right principle of individuation to be a person. There is room in the world for both persons and bodies, however, and enough matter for both. Since their matter must be the same there is no question of competition or displacement between them. *Lebensraum* is an ecological problem which ontology cannot aggravate.

APPENDIX

Some residual problems about sortal concepts

As the book goes to press I notice a number of points on which I shall have perplexed or misled the reader. I take this opportunity to anticipate some misunderstandings, appropriate a number of criticisms and slightly modify some conclusions.

5.1. It is fairly consistently supposed in the body of the text that it will be a matter of the *sense* of a sortal expression whether it expresses a phase-concept or a substance-concept (e.g. p. 30, fn. 40); and again (p. 32) that it is the mission of the *sense* of a substance-concept f to fix in a schematic and general way the persistence conditions for fs. It may be asked how, if this were so, men could ever have *discovered* for example (what remained unknown for centuries) that a certain class of elvers, *Leptocephali*, long supposed to be a separate species, were in fact the young of the species *Conger Eel*, that tadpoles become frogs, and so on.

An idealized and overschematic answer to this question might be this. Language can stably accommodate porous or indeterminate sortal concepts f, which enable us to pick out fs during some stretch of their existence and which leave quite open the character of fs during other periods of their life-history. These porous sortal concepts would not yet have the determinate character of phase-concepts. (For a phase-concept f, strictly so qualifying, has it as part of its sense—does not merely leave room for the possibility—that it restricts a wider sortal-concept g. Thus g determines or partially determines the limits within which a g can persist through change both inside and outside an f phase.) The account would go on to suggest that when a thinker is equipped with such a porous sortal concept f and has the *general* concept of a continuant through change (or, if you will, has the capacity to quantify over substance-concepts), then if he wishes (or if he is constrained by analogy with what he already does in other cases) the thinker can count a suitable event or process which he witnesses befall an f as the discovery that fs *become* f's.

With this decision comes the possibility of building it into the sense of f that f is a restriction of some wider sortal-concept g, and of determining that both f and f' are phase-sortals. With this enlargement of knowledge of *what* fs *are* there would then come the possibility of the invention or discovery of concept g, and of a genuine modification of the concept of an f. And here for once there could be a genuine modification of sense, the modification of the sense of the expression standing for the sortal-concept f. It will lose some or all of its porosity.

There is nothing at all disturbing about the trivial courtesy title of *necessary a posteriori* which by this account such a discovery and decision confer upon e.g. the proposition that all fs are gs. What gives the proposition this force is unmysterious. We can also see what would force us to give up the invented concept g and the newly determined concept f and prompt us to retreat to the old porous concept of an f. We also understand what sorts of consideration would support or undermine the decision to make it taxonomically definitive of gs that they had phases in which they were fs and f's. The considerations are familiar enough.

This account is far too schematic, and it is hopelessly artificial to suggest that questions of sense can be so easily separated from questions of fact. But it gives a schema which can be varied and sophisticated to articulate detailed narrations of actual case histories from science and of discoveries in real life; and it serves to alert us to the porosity of many of the sortal concepts which we actually employ (Cp. fn. 37 end).

5.2. The complexity of the counting thesis C, as stated on page 1, gives rise to the possibility of a serious ambiguity of intention in Part Two. For of course identity-statements can be covered by concepts for particulars which, by certain strict standards, nobody would be entirely happy to call substances. *Oily wave* (p. 39) is such, as would be *volume of argon, area of garden,* etc. So for all I have said it *may* still be that countability is a condition of substancehood in some very strict sense of substance which I leave it to those enamoured of it to describe. (But the distinction at p. 39 remains, between the requirement of saying 'one' or 'two' for x and y, fs identified and referred to in a context, and the problematic requirement of a general method of enumerating fs.) Part Two simply exploits the truism that sortal concepts cover identities to get conditions of being a substance in the loose sense *individual decomposable into matter*. *Strict* substances need further conditions.

5.3. I am still inclined to accept Williams' hard requirement that coincidence-type sufficient conditions of identity must be genuinely *sufficient* (p. 37–8, fn. 47, fn. 48, fn. 38, p. 52 foll.), to make the distinction at p. 43 between criteria and tests, and to insist that we must have the *criterion* before the question can arise of any *test* of identity. (For the test has to be a test of the satisfaction of that criterion to be a test of *identity*). Anyone who finds this hard line repellent can and must still accept (D. ix.). He can, because it is *coincidence under f* as a whole which is concerned, and he can build the satisfaction of any *ceteris paribus* clauses by which he sets store into the force of the *coincidence* element in *coincidence under f*. (And one can even build into it what I recently heard Miss J. M. Rountree call a 'bet', the bet that *cetera* will be *paria*).

5.4. Williams has asked me of what concept the concept *person* could on my account be (in the sense of page 30) the restriction. If the Lockean conception of a person and emphasis on experience-memory and continuity of consciousness are pushed to the length of making a radical distinction between persons and other animals, the latter being regarded simply as living-bodies, then the unguarded answer that *person* straightforwardly restricts *animal* may seem to threaten me either with the logical possibility of a case of R or with the resurgence of Williams' simple bodily criterion, which I had intended to supersede. (For the sort of force which Williams might intend by the hyphenation of 'living-body' see p. 49.) *Person* in my use is certainly a (non-biological) qualification of *animal*. Indeed I am fully prepared for it to turn out to be, in some sense, a cross-classification with respect to zoological classifications, and to include dolphins, porpoises, etc. Even, in exchange for suitably amazing behaviour (suitably explained in neurophysiological terms), to include a parrot. If so, it will certainly follow that a person is an animal who has, or has the biological capacity for, experience-memory, sufficient self-awareness, etc. But if *animal*, which *person* qualifies in this way, already by itself had an autonomous individuative force which was simply equivalent to that of *living-body* then either body-continuity would have to arbitrate all identity-questions about persons or we should again have the logical possibility of a case of R.

There are two complementary answers to the difficulty, of which the second is more fundamental. The first answer might be to refuse to equate the meaning of 'animal' with that of 'living-body', adapt the individuative procedure of Part Four to some creatures which we do not account persons, and to extend this procedure as far down the evolutionary tree as there remain 'psychologically' interesting functional differences between different members of any one species of animal. But secondly and more fundamentally, *animal* is not really individuative in quite the same way as *horse, cat, man*, or *person* are. What coincidence under the concept *animal* amounts to *differs according to the kind of animal.* The genus-sortal is in this sense less fundamental than the species-sortal. I ought not to have left undeveloped the distinction adverted to at the end of footnote 40, nor been so happy to allow that the restriction of substance- or species-concepts was the same as the restriction of genus-concepts. It is not quite the same.

With this conclusion I take one more step along the same 'essentialist' path as Aristotle. But my starting point was utterly extensional. It was Leibniz and the rejection of *qua* (p. 23). And nothing so far said need lead to Aristotle's idolatry of the *species* in particular. (An insecure concept in plant-taxonomy, and threatened even in zoology by such phenomena as ring-species and the imperfect transitivity of the relation *interbreeds in the wild with*—the operational test of identity of species.) What does now receive a privileged status is the highest genuine sortal concept g_n in any chain of restrictions, $g_1, g_2, \ldots$ which carries with it an autonomous individuative force sufficient to determine without reference to lower sortals the coincidence and persistence conditions for any g. (I should surmise that g_n may possibly be nothing other than a concept which is ultimate in the sense of p. 32). On all these questions cp. Leibniz *Nouveaux Essais* 3.3.6.

This is not quite the end of the answer to Williams' question. If *person* might cross-classify *human being* and (say) *dolphin* then, by the doctrine of pages 32–4, either the cross-classification must be resolved in some one sortal classification, genuine and higher, of both men and dolphins, or *person* is not a *sortal* cross-classification.

It is perfectly possible to cope with both horns of this dilemma. If someone chooses to deny that the cross-classification can be resolved then the answer to the second is this. *Person* may be a concept which only becomes fully determinate as an individuative concept when one is told *what sort of person*, e.g. *man*-person or (if there really were such things) *dolphin*-person. It is only in this way, after all, that ordinary very high genera such as *animal* can be said to individuate individuals or give covering concepts for their identities. At risk of multiplying terminology one might call such concepts *sortal-schemata*, and such not strictly sortal cross-classification *schematic*.

5.5. All this leads on to an oversight in the proof at page 33. It might happen that g_1 and h_1 were so related that nothing *could* be both a g_1 and an h_1. The possibility is not interesting of course in that context—a proof that one individual which is *already* cross-classified as a g_1 and an h_1 must fall under some substance-concept throughout its existence—but it has to be considered in order to secure full generality. Now in this case, which I overlooked, the formula on line 12 would be vacuously satisfied by falsity of the antecedent, and g_1 and h_1 would determine disjoint classes. No question of a case of R or of branching identities need then begin to arise. But it remains true that *either* f_1 and h_1 will nevertheless fall under a single sortal principle *or* f'' will have no claim to be a *unitary* sortal with fully determined individuative force which determines continuity and persistence-conditions for f''s in one way.

5.6. On the subject of footnote 55, it is much more important to show the 'effectiveness' of my criterion of coincidence for persons than to vindicate my rather dubious machine example. But it surely is effective. Consider the following grossly over-simplified procedure. Start where you will in the life of person f. Suppose f witnesses or participates in event e. Then at the next stage search for the g, if there is one, which carries the material and causal trace of the right sort of experiencing of e. Even if we do need help here from the concept of *body* that is no reason why *person* should not be defined by a rule for the systematic modification (*not* the restriction) of the concept *body*, provided the modification is not specified in a way which makes the task of tracing a person and the criterion for *same person* non-effective, regressive or circular. The store we set by continuity of consciousness is what prompts us to have amongst others this kind of concept. (See again p. 57).

5.7. I did not sufficiently plainly distinguish as different two quite different ways in which a person Jones might degenerate into a 'concrete universal'. If social pressure builds up for a qualitatively suitable actor for a certain role and this pressure is sustained by a judge's decision (say in an inheritance suit), then *one* way (certainly not the best) of describing the decision is in terms of a quasi-universal Jones. This establishes nothing whatever about co-consciousness or continuity of consciousness and it is quite different from the more interesting clone-universal thrown up by the grafted vegetative continuity of all Cox's Orange Pippin trees with the original tree, or the causal memory-continuity of Brown I and Brown II with Brown.

NOTES TO THE TEXT

[1] Some may hold that the reverse dependence exists between the two doctrines. Others may hold that they are equivalent doctrines. But the supposition that D depends for its cogency on its being possible for *a* to be the same f and not the same g as *b* is certainly made by both P. T. Geach and W. V. Quine in recent controversy about these matters. (It looks as if something like this is also supposed by V. Chappell, in his otherwise incontrovertible 'Sameness & Change', *Phil. Rev.*, vol. LXIX (Jan. 1960), p. 359, lines 12–13). Professor Geach insists on the legitimacy of always pressing the *same what*? demand (see *Reference and Generality*, Ithaca, N.Y., Cornell 1962, §31–§34 and Chapter Six), and one of his arguments for it, at least in conversation and correspondence, is certainly provided by the doctrine that it is logically possible for *a* to be the same f as *b* without being the same g as *b*. Professor Quine in his review of *Reference and Generality* (*Philosophical Review*, vol. LXXII (Jan. 1964), p. 102) rejects out of hand the possibility of *a* being the same f as *b* without being the same g as *b*, and it is apparently *on the strength of that rejection* that he strongly questions the legitimacy of always pressing Geach's *same what*? demand and questions the necessity for Geach's many-sorted treatment of the predicate-calculus. The one point on which Geach and Quine seem to be agreed is that it is the possibility of *a's* being the same f but not the same g as *b* which provides the principal rationale of D.

[2] The Lockean term *sortal* is used in roughly the manner of the second part of P. F. Strawson's *Individuals* (Methuen London 1956). See especially pp. 168–169.

[3] This title is suggested by Quine's review, op. cit., p. 102, and his characterization of the *Reference and Generality* doctrine (a doctrine which comes out at e.g. p. 157, where Geach says 'I could not object in principle to different As being one and the same B; and thus different intentional objects [*if* one could at all accept such things] could be one and the same man, as different official personages may be one and the same man').

[4] For other recent support of D (D for requirement of *Definiteness*) or for related theses see e.g. A. Prior, *Analysis*, vol. 17 (June 1957); S. Hampshire, 'Identification and Existence' in *Contemporary British Philosophy* (Third series, London 1956) ed. H. D. Lewis; D. Wiggins, 'Individuation of Things and Places', P.A.S. Supp. XXXVIII (1963), p. 126.

[5] C is commonly supposed to give not only a sufficient but a necessary condition of being a sortal-concept (Cp. Strawson, *Individuals*, loc. cit. See also my 'Individuation', op. cit., which is mistaken on this point.)

[6] On the suggestion of Mr. Wilfrid Hodges of New College, Oxford, to whom I am extremely grateful for this and for other suggestions.

[7] See the end of section 6 of this Part (page 15), and in section 7 of this Part the discussion of (λ) (page 20). Amendments of Leibniz' Law designed to save R are also considered in connexion with (λ). All objections to construing identity as a function now seem to me quite ineffective.

[8] Sometimes referred to as 'strict' or 'absolute' identity. I don't object to this description provided it be not understood as committing me to believing in the coherence (which is doubtful, see below the discussion of (λ), pp. 20-5) of a 'less than strict' or a 'relative' notion of identity. By 'strict identity', if I were obliged under threats to use the phrase, I should certainly not mean an identity-concept which excluded the possibility of asking *same* or *identical what*? So far as I can see there is

no such identity-concept for substances. I shall contend that it is precisely the possibility of answering the *same what* question by means of a substance-term that makes this 'strict' or Leibnizian notion of identity applicable to changing and persisting things.

⁹ Indeed, together with reflexivity, Leibniz' Law entails the other properties. See Quine, *Set Theory and Its Logic* (Belknap, Harvard, Cambridge, Mass., 1964), p. 13. Nevertheless, for reasons which Quine gives (compare *From a Logical Point of View* Harvard, 1953, pp. 70 f., 117 f.) and which Geach has elaborated and impressed upon me, neither a relation R's satisfying the schema $((\exists f)(a = b)) \supset (Fa \equiv Fb)$ nor

its satisfying the schema $Fy \equiv (\exists x)$ $(xRy$ & $Fx)$ completely ties that relation down within a first order formal system to what we normally intend by identity. This does not weaken the claim that we need *at least* Leibniz' Law to mark off what is peculiar to identity. We do. Cp. Frege's remark in his review of Husserl, page 80 in Geach & Black's *Translations from the Philosophical Writings of Gottlob Frege* (Oxford Blackwell's, 1952), 'I agree . . . that Leibniz's explanation *eadem sunt quorum unum potest substitui alteri salva veritate* does not deserve to be called a definition; my reasons, however, are different from Husserl's. Since any definition is an identity, identity itself cannot be defined. This explanation of Leibniz's could be called an axiom that brings out the nature of the relation of identity; as such it is fundamentally important'. Frege here lumps what I have called Leibniz' Law together with its converse, the suspect Identity of Indiscernibles, and the doctrine of definition seems dubious, but for the left to right reading which yields the substitutivity principle, his contention still seems to me compelling. See also *Grundgesetze der Arithmetik* (Jena 1903), II Band, 254.

Some assaults on Leibniz' Law would bring transitivity down with it too (See A. N. Prior 'Time, Existence, and Identity' P.A.S. LXVII (1965–6), p. 188), and leave us knowing dangerously little about the notion of identity.

At risk of tedium I fear I must reiterate my warning in the Introduction that there is a very great deal to be said about Leibniz' Law which I make no attempt to say in this monograph. Any complete vindication of my use of it would involve e.g. discussion of the specification of relevant predicables and discussion of whether these could be specified absolutely without danger of paradox. It would also involve discussion of uses which an opponent might make of Quine's notion of relative discernibility. (See *Word and Object*, New York 1960, page 230.)

¹⁰ In 'On Sense and Reference' reprinted in Geach and Black's *Translations*. Frege's arguments do of course stand in need of expansion and development, and Church's two proposals for this are by no means the only ones which could be made. The notion of *actual*, as opposed to *apparent*, reference, and Frege's distinction between the occurrence of an expression with its *direct* and its occurrence with its *indirect* sense, require considerable sophistication. Here I can only say that I am confident that the substance of Frege's proposal can be preserved, and that it can be preserved within a perfectly common sense account of what it is for a sentence to be *about* something. Considerations (i) and (iii) fortify my certainty that this must be so.

¹¹ *Mind*, vol. LXXIII (October 1964).

¹² Op. cit., p. 151.

¹³ Hume, *Treatise* I.4 (p. 244 in the Everyman edition).

¹⁴ Cp. Geach, op. cit., p. 157.

¹⁵ Cp. Locke, *Essay*, II, XXVIII,   9 and 23.

¹⁶ I realize that I here present anybody who thinks they have a clear concept of identity which is independent of Leibniz' Law with an unusually good fund of

'counter-examples' to that Law. I hereby challenge them to provide an account of the formal properties of their notion of identity, and to accommodate most or all of this ragbag of examples (and also (μ) below, perhaps) under a single umbrella of straightforward 'identity'. If any substantial number of them be rejected then my opponent will be already engaged on what I shall be engaged in, the discovery of those sorts of alternative analysis which, in my treatment, discredit all the type-(4) and type-(5) pretensions of examples (α)–(μ).

[17] The principle that if a is the same as b then a must exist at those and only those times at which b exists is not an uncontentious substitution-instance of Leibniz' Law. That depends on whether or not tensed existence is a genuine predicate of individuals. Geach and Anscombe have argued that tensed existence, which they distinguish from the non-tensed existence represented by the existential quantifier, is a genuine predicate. (Since they treat Leibniz' Law with suspicion the same questions do not hang on this for them as hang on it for an upholder of the Law.) But if it is not a predicate (which, for reasons I cannot here go into, I am still inclined to suppose it is not) then analogous doubts will arise about such grammatical predicates as *create*, *make*, *produce*, *fabricate*, *destroy*, and even *break* (though none would arise for a predicate I could have used in the text to make my case, *repair* or *replace a part of*); they too would fail to qualify as straightforward substitution instances of the predicate variable, ϕ, in Leibniz' Law. Leaving this question open, I shall simply say (i) that even if the requirement of identity of life-histories and durations is not a substitution instance of Leibniz' Law it is nevertheless self-evidently true; and (ii) that it ought to be indirectly derivable from the Law without the use of the dubious substitution. Suppose that a were identical with b, that a existed at t_i and that b did not exist at t_i. This difference between a and b would have to reflect a difference in the genuine predicates true of a and b at t_i. But any such difference in genuine predicates would be disallowed by Leibniz' Law. It is precisely one part of the Russellian and Fregean view that existence is not a predicate that (a exists at t). $\supset$. ($\exists \phi$) (a is ϕ at t), that (a exists at t).$\equiv$. ($\exists$ f) (a is f at t), and indeed that, for all those predicates ϕ which qualify a thing present-tensedly only during its existence (a exists at t)$\equiv$(a is ϕ at t). Indeed Russell's view would be that there was something ill-formed about 'a exists at t' and that it should be everywhere supplanted by one of the above right hand side implications or equivalents. It is certainly an extraordinarily bizarre idea that the coffee pot could have been identical with the heap of fragments and so taken up room, the room they took up, but not existed. It makes it sound as if a passenger could travel from St. Pancras to Glasgow without a railway ticket on a sleeping car reservation alone. I should be grateful to be told how this is legally done. In a box (State funeral)?

[18] A principle none the less true for having prompted false theories of predication, e.g. Antisthenes' identity-theory. See Aristotle *Metaphysics* 1024^{b32} or Hobbes *De Corpore* I. 3.2. It implies no such absurdity.

[19] I am not saying that the possibility of this paraphrase by itself forces us to postulate this distinct sense of 'is'. I am saying that the independent plausibility of this paraphrase, *plus* the plausibility of Leibniz' Law which would otherwise have to be amended or abandoned, *plus* the difficulty of amending Leibniz' Law, force us to postulate this distinct sense of 'is'.

[20] 'If we burn down all the trees of a wood we thereby burn down the wood'. Thus [in the concrete sense of class] there can be no empty class'. Frege's review of Schroeder's *Algebra der Logik* in Geach and Black's *Translations*, p. 89.

[21] Ibidem, p. 87.

[22] For a description of mereology (the calculus of individuals) see A. Tarski, 'Foundation of Geometry of Solids' in *Logic Semantics and Metamathematics* (Oxford,

1956), p. 24, or Nelson Goodman's *Structure of Appearance* (Harvard, Cambridge, 1951), chap. 2. See also J. H. Woodger *The Axiomatic Method in Biology* (Cambridge 1937), Chapter III, Section 1, and Appendix E (by Tarski), p. 161.

²³ The definition of 'Y is disjoint from Z' is 'no individual W is a part both of Y and Z'. The reference to classes in the definition of *sum of elements* is eliminable (as is indicated by the square bracketing). The 'part of' relation is transitive in mereology.

²⁴ The difficulty is not so quickly evaded as it might seem. It is very difficult to see how exactly one could redefine the Leśniewskian whole of J without including J as a part of J, and even if it were possible it would not be enough. For one cannot destroy the *improper* part of J without affecting *proper* parts of J and doing something just as drastic to them as to J. For to shatter J, or even break it into two, is to shatter the indefinite, even potentially infinite, number of proper parts of it which lie across the break.

²⁵ See Carnap's *Introduction to Symbolic Logic and Its Applications* (Dover edition, New York, 1958), p. 157 following, p. 198, and p. 213 following.

²⁶ Still a doubt may persist. Isn't the life-histories principle too strong? Might not the jug be identical with a stretch of some Leśniewskian whole X for such time as no part of the jug is broken or replaced? But quite apart from the support we have adduced for the strict life-histories principle, this 'temporary identity' is surely a very peculiar sort of identity. We surely cannot give a sense to the supposition that Hesperus might be the same planet as Phosphorus for a bit and then stop being Phosphorus. But then the relation between the jug and the redefined whole X looks as if it cannot be the same sort of relation as that between Hesperus and Phosphorus. The conclusion for which I am arguing is of course just this, that they are related by the one being composed or constituted of the other, not by identity.

Definite descriptions can qualify objects temporarily, but the support they give to 'temporary *identity*' is quite illusory. See D. Wiggins 'Identity-Statements' in *Analytical Philosophy* (Second Series, ed. R. J. Butler, Blackwell, Oxford, 1965, pp. 42–46, the only part of that article of which I should now wish to offer much defence).

²⁷ Which is surely at least a part of a completely satisfactory theory of proper names, one which could in fact be defended against Linsky all the more effectively if my general thesis were correct.

²⁸ Thus perhaps 'The same sovereign was a man, is now a woman' need not signify that anybody has changed their sex (unless 'anybody' be thought of as adapted to perform precisely the same trick as 'sovereign').

²⁹ Cp. Quine's objection (review cit.) to Geach's argument at *Reference and Generality*, p. 151.

³⁰ It is enough here that such a distinction between genuine and pseudo-predicates is needed. Its exact formulation (see e.g. Ayer 'Identity of Indiscernibles' in *Philosophical Essays*, or part VI of my 'Individuation of Things and Places' op. cit., p. 193) is difficult but not here important.

It is in fact an analytic consequence of the account of identity in Part Two that coinciding *under a covering concept* at a time and place settles an identity-question, and with it of course the numerical question 'how many persons are *a* and *b*?'

³¹ See Quine's review op. cit., for a general rebuttal of an objection in *Reference and Generality* to this kind of argument.

³² This will lead to a division of predicates similar to one which Hodges pointed out to me that Pope Leo made in his *Tome* of 449.

'Deus per id quod omnia per ipsum facta sunt et sine ipso factum est nihil;

homo per id quod factus est ex muliere, factus sub lege . . . esurire, sitire, lassescere atque dormire evidenter humanum est.'

[33] I owe reference to an example which falls outside these three kinds to Professor Geach and Miss Anscombe, both of whom very kindly read an earlier version of part of this monograph and gave it the most searching criticisms. I am also greatly indebted to Professor Geach for correspondence on some related matters, e.g. footnote (7). Neither Professor Geach nor Miss Anscombe is of course responsible for any of the mistakes to be found here, and both would strenuously oppose many of the conclusions I persist in detaching by the use of Leibniz' Law.

The example is to be found in Aristotle *Physics* 202^b. Consider the road from Athens to Thebes. It is the same road as the road Thebes to Athens. But the road Athens-Thebes is uphill and the road Thebes-Athens is downhill. My objection to counting this example (*qua* Athens-Thebes uphill, *qua* Thebes-Athens downhill) is that either 'road' means an actual feature of the landscape, in which case 'uphill' collects a term giving the direction and there is a simple relational predicate true of that road, or it means 'journey by road', in which case there is no identity.

[34] Why be content with one *qua* f once one has got started? If Jesus Christ could teach the doctors at the age of twelve then he was by that age good *qua* scholar, that is to say a good scholar. This he was *qua* man. This he was perhaps *qua* person, not *qua* God. . . . How in general do we know when we have enough *quas*? And when we know that we have, why shouldn't we transfer the whole compound predicate by the orthodox Leibniz' Law?

[35] Hilary Putnam calls something similar 'theoretical identification'. See his essay in *Dimensions of Mind* ed. Sidney Hook, (New York, 1960), p. 169. See now also the end of Paul Benacerraf's 'What Numbers Couldn't Be' in *Philosophical Review* XXIV (January 1965), for a very similar conclusion.

[36] 'Function and Concept' in Geach and Black, *op. cit.*, p. 32.

[37] And nothing in the proof must depend on a certain conceptual conservatism into which no philosophical inquiry into substance and identity should find itself forced, viz. the supposition that one can tell *a priori* for any given sortal, e.g. the sortal *tadpole* or *pupa*, whether or not it is a substance-sortal or merely a phase-sortal. Room must be found for the empirical and surprising discovery that there is something which is first a tadpole and then a frog—one might designate what goes through the whole cycle, what becomes *this* and then turns into *that*, *batrachos*—or is first a pupa or chrysalis and then becomes a perfect insect. The proof which follows leaves room for that.

'Another type of linguistic shortcoming [in biology] is illustrated by the persistence of our tendency to identify *organisms* with *adults* . . . it is not just adults we classify when we classify organisms. . . . We can speak of the egg as the primordium of the future adult, but not of the future organism because it already is the organism'. J. H. Woodger 'On Biological Transformation' in *Growth and Form*, Essays for D'Arcy Thompson (edited Le Gros Clark and Medawar) Oxford, 1945.

When we invent a sortal we may not have enough information to invent a substance-sortal. We may have to content ourselves with a phase-sortal and incomplete or indeterminate persistence-conditions. And there are many sortals in use about whose status we have not bothered to ask ourselves.

[38] No good to say f' will do provided that it has no competition from some g. For if 'b coincides under f' with c_1' is grounds for '$b \underset{f'}{=} c$' then it must still be grounds

for that, even if b also coincides under g with c_2. For

$$(p \Rightarrow q) \supset ((p \ \& \ r) \Rightarrow q).$$

Nor will it do to say this competition cannot arise because of Leibniz' Law. See the

F

discussion of (D.ix) below. All that Leibniz' Law secures is that if the claims of each side are equally strong then both *lose*. It is an *adequacy condition* of our individuative practices and our sortal concepts that they should preserve the formal properties of identity. Leibniz' Law cannot itself prevent sloppy individuative practices or ill-defined sortals from running into logical difficulty. The boot is on the other foot. Our individuative practices are only genuinely *individuative* if they are so regulated as to preserve the formal properties of identity. For *identity criterion* see p. 43.

[39] If such structures were set up by Plato's method of dichotomous division then that would of course ensure that h_1 and g_1 each fell under some higher genus g_n or under its complement not-g_n; and if all divisions were properly dichotomous then all the classes separated on any level would be disjoint and f'' simply could not fall under the overlapping classes g_1 and h. Indeed the whole structure would then be instantly recognisable as a topological tree, or in Woodger's sense, a hierarchy. Any two sortals which occurred on it would either determine disjoint classes or determine classes such that one was wholly included in the other; and for any pair of classes so related by inclusion there would be a class which was included in the includer but was included in no other class included in the includer. (Woodger in *The Axiomatic Method*, op. cit., p. 42, defines a hierarchy as a relation R which is asymmetrical, one-many, has one and only one beginner, and is such that its converse domain is identical with the terms to which the beginner stands in some power of R.) But this gain is quite illusory if it is achieved by dichotomy. You cannot say what a thing is by saying what it is not, so at least half of the terms on such a tree would not be sortals; this and the other objections have been well-known since Aristotle (cf. *De Partibus Animalium* 642^{b5} foll.), indeed since Plato (cp. *Politicus* 262^D). See p. 121 ff. of H. W. B. Joseph's *Introduction to Logic* (2nd Edition, Oxford 1916).

That zoological sortals form or come near to forming such a strict hierarchy has only to do with the evolutionary character of the material the taxonomist has always been called upon to bring into order. This character had after all to be stamped deep enough on it to cause Darwin and Wallace to discover the theory of evolution at all, and the presence of the character had always in fact conditioned the labours of taxonomists, even those who had no inkling of the theory, and regardless of non-evolutionary or anti-evolutionary orientation. The hierarchical arrangement of zoological sortals rests on a wholly contingent fact, the one-many property within the subject-matter of pre- or post-Darwinian taxonomy of the relation 'evolves into' in the field of animal species. (Even here sibling species such as the notorious fruit flies, *Drosophila Pseudoobscura* and *Drosophila Persimilis* may count as constituting a kind of exception. And it is not logically impossible, even if it is genetically utterly inconceivable, that the phenomenon of convergence within quite diverse species, even say species of orders as remote as *marsupial* and *rodent*, should give rise to the same difficulty). It has absolutely nothing to do with any use of a method of dichotomy or any specifically *logical* objections to cross-classification as such. Although zoology provides the most imposing and striking example of a system of sortal classification, its rather special formal character has over-impressed and misled philosophers and logicians.

A case where cross-classification is indispensable, and indispensable for compelling theoretical reasons is this:

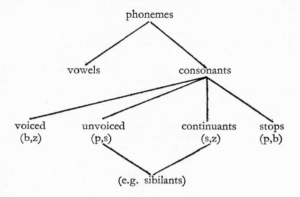

There is no way of rearranging this to expel cross-classifications and achieve the identificatory advantages of a 'key' without breaking up theoretically significant groups. (Cf. p. 80 of Noam Chomsky *Aspects of the Theory of Syntax* (M.I.T. Cambridge, Massachussets, 1965).)

[40] That there must be such an ultimate sortal seems to flow from an *a priori* principle of *Definiteness of Classification* comparable to the *Tractatus* requirement of *Definiteness of Sense*—indeed it might be seen as a special case of that—or even to Mirimanoff's requirement of *Foundation* or *Regularity* for sets (a requirement which excludes any set x_1 below which there extends an infinite descending sequence of sets $(x_2 \varepsilon x_1)$ and $(x_3 \varepsilon x_2)$ and $(x_4 \varepsilon x_3)$ and ..). Sortals are by definition concepts which classify. If f_1 restricted f_2, and f_2 restricted f_3, and f_3 restricted ... and so indefinitely, and if the sense of each of the members of the chain required allusion to the next member, then until we were assured that there was something which they all ultimately restricted, $f_1, f_2, f_3,..$ could not in the final analysis *classify* anything at all. For there would be nothing definite of which this infinite chain of sortals could be the determinate specifications.

If f_n is an ultimate sortal in the sense of ultimacy defined in the text it does not follow that f_n restricts no further sortal. In the case where it does it will simply not be a part of its *sense* that it restricts a further sortal. Perhaps species-sortals are ultimate in the sense defined—though nothing so far said will show this—but these do of course restrict wider genus-concepts. The relation of phase-sortal to substance-sortal and the relation of species to genus are rather different relations but nothing in the foregoing argument hangs on what exactly the difference is which we encounter at the point when we pass on our way upwards in a restriction diagram from the one to the other. Both relations, phase-sortal to substance-sortal and species to genus, determine subrelations of the relation 'f_i restricts f_j' and so of the relation 'subset of'.

[41] See Strawson *op. cit.* p. 122–3 and Section VI of my 'Identification of Things and Places', cited in footnote 4, and also Section VIII *ibidem*.

[42] 'Individuation of Things and Places', *op. cit.*, p. 176 following, where an apparent circularity in this account is discussed.

[43] Identification, distinctness, and reidentification have to boil down to much the same thing for the special case of persisting material things, which is all we are here treating. See Section V of my *op. cit.* page 189 and M. J. Woods' article 'Identity and Individuation' in *Analytical Philosophy* (Second Series, Blackwell, Oxford, 1965).

[44] It might be said that it was not necessary—all that was necessary was to find a and b in the same place at the same time. But first, how can we know what it is to find a in a place unless we have *some* sortal specification of what a is. Second, the assertion that a and b coincide must come to something more than the stale assertion that the location of a = the location of b. It is the *occupants* or things associated with the place which must be the same. We must know not only what is for location l to be *occupied* but also what it is for l to be occupied *by a*. a's continued occupation of l cannot be verified, for instance, by the fact that other things cannot be pushed into l. Apart from the possible circularity of this acount, we should still have no determinate way of tracing a and isolating a from something else, x, which moved up to a and then moved into l while a moved out of l. A thing is not the same as its location. Now to teach someone to isolate or (where applicable) trace a under a substance-concept cannot possibly be a separate matter from teaching him what it is for a to coincide with a'. If a and a' genuinely coincide they will *ipso facto* both fit under one individuative or identificatory genus and D will *ipso facto* have applied to the case. If they do not do so we shall not obviously have more than the stale assertion that their locations are the same.

It may be counter-objected that if a and a' are in exactly the same place at the same time they must be identical. But consider examples (α) and (β) of Part One. It is analytic in virtue of T that x and y cannot be in the same place at the same time where x and y are subsumable under one sortal. But any case my opponent and I are arguing about is *ex hypothesi* not a case where there is one relevant sortal or where T applies.

Locke gets this absolutely right at Essay II. XXVIII. 1: 'we never finding, nor conceiving it possible, that two things *of the same kind* should exist in the same place at the same time, we rightly conclude, that whatever exists anywhere at any time, excludes *all of the same kind*, and is there itself alone'.

The covering concept-requirement necessarily affects general identity statements and (since, as already remarked, all ϕ's are ψ's implies every ϕ is identical to some ψ) straightforward general predications. Such statements as 'genes are DNA molecules' might be thought to constitute an apparent exception to the requirement. The exception is only apparent. I think it will be seen that what is happening here is that 'gene' means *whatever it is* that accounts for (such and such) facts of heredity'; and that the whole sentence reduces in any case, for anybody with any kind of sympathy for a Russellian theory of reference, to 'DNA molecules account for such and such facts of heredity'. For such statements as 'numbers are classes of classes', see again the discussion of (μ) and the reference to Benacerraf.

[45] *De Corpore* II.11 (Molesworth, p. 136).

[46] It is a peculiarity of mereology, if the principle that $(a=b). \equiv . [(a$ is a part of $b)$ & (b is a part of a)] were not excluded from operating through time, that it would favour the plank-hoarder's reconstructed ship.

[47] It is precisely this which non-bodily concepts of person seem to fail to do. Cp. Williams' discussion in 'Personal Identity and Individuation' P.A.S. LVII (1956–7). See also his 'Personal Identity and Continuity' Analysis 20, 2 (December, 1960). My debt to both of these publications will be manifest. The requirement in the text can be interpreted strictly enough, though it is an open question whether it ought, to entail precisely the conclusion Williams draws, that no substantial discontinuities in the material presence of a material individual a can be allowed.

(See also fn. 38 p. 43). If reappearance after a gap of suitable a' could imply or ground the conclusion that $a = a'$ then so would the situation: *suitable reappearance of a'* and p. For, again, $(r \Rightarrow q) \supset (p \ \& \ r \Rightarrow q)$. But what if p assumes the value 'suitable a'' has also appeared, and $a' \neq a''$?' Sufficient conditions are *sufficient* conditions.

see erratum note, p viii.

It may be objected that all that Williams has shown is that to get a genuinely sufficient condition of identity we must gloss 'suitable reappearance of a'' so that it *entails* the absence of competitors. 'Suitable a'' has also appeared and $a' \neq a'''$ would then be self-contradictory. I cannot go into this fully here but would simply remark that it looks to me like an unpromising manoeuvre. For on the view then propounded there would have to figure among the grounds for '$a = a'$' a proposition of unlimited generality about the whole universe, viz. that there was no competitor *anywhere* to be found, nor presumably *at any time* any competitor which could not be fitted into the history of a without breach of transitivity. I do not believe that '$a = a'$' has such a close resemblance to a general proposition. There is also a suspicion of circularity. Admittedly we have in Leibniz' Law an independent criterion sufficient to distinguish a' and a'' from one another and to rule that they are compertitors for identity with a. But this criterion of difference only works if they are qualitatively distinguishable. If they are not, then one criterion of difference is their *non-coincidence*. On pain of regress, however, this has to be a failure to coincide in the straightforward sense described and defended in the text, which throws the objector back on the interpretation of coincidence and non-coincidence. Alternatively a' and a'' might be distinguished by place. But that throws us back again onto a framework of material things which would have to be individuated by a criterion of straightforward coincidence of the kind which I have defended.

[48] Contrast Prior op. cit. footnote 7. The decision in the text conforms with the only thorough attempt to work out a logic of division and fusion, that of J. H. Woodger, p. 61, op. cit. footnote 20.

[49] It is sometimes objected that we must have disjunctive sortals for certain kinds of counting operation, but 'There are 26 women *or* shadows in the room' means, obviously, 'The number of women *plus* the number of shadows = 26'. We do not need disjunctive sortals to find our way here. Perhaps it will be well to reiterate that this is not an argument against essentially disjunctive f *or* g being a concept. It is an argument against its being a *sortal* concept.

[50] *De Corpore* II. 8.1.

[51] E.g. Frege *Grundgesetze der Arithmetik* Vol. II, sections 56–67, whose insistence that the right hand must know what the left hand is doing is no less important as a regulative principle of correctness for discoveries about sound concepts in use than it is indispensable as a rule for the legitimate and non-creative introduction of concepts into a formalized language. It is an extraordinary idea that one could just 'read off' principles of personal identity from a series of decisions which were given *in extenso*. Even if necessarily most or all of them were correct decisions, there are too many different principles one might claim to discern there. If an unprecedented situation arises this may perhaps lead to the abandonment of a concept. Or it may lead to a new decision which may upset previous philosophical ideas about the rules for the concept's application. If the new decision is a coherent one then that discredits the philosophical ideas. It *need* not import a new concept or change people's ideas about the rules and criteria for the concept's application. For people do not standardly have any such ideas formulated or formulable. They simply have an understanding of the *point* of the application of the concept. And the point of what they do after the new decision will usually be continuous with the point of what they did before it. They will still mean the same by 'person'. The only people who have formulated ideas about criteria are philosophers. But these ideas are fallible and they

cannot float free of logical constraint, or of Frege's requirements of soundness for concepts. (Unless these philosophers believe the concept unsound. But then they must *prove* that it cannot have any consistent rules of application.)

What is compelling in Frege's critique of piecemeal definition does not by itself imply the full rigour of Leśniewski's requirements for definition, which are too strict and would gravely threaten the admissibility of vague or partially defined concepts. Consistency is what matters. Sufficient conditions may be provably consistent without implying anything about the impossibility of vague cases or about *tertium non datur*. And one can have a very precise understanding of the application and point of a vague concept, and be pretty sure that it is not contradictory or paradoxical. Vague concepts are perfectly all right as they are. If a good sortal is vague that only means that there are some borderline cases to decide—under constraints, even here. *Pace* Reid, vague concepts are not even necessarily concepts which admit of degrees. Nor are the good ones ambiguous. Nor are they unformalizable.

My remarks about the relevance and importance of Frege's and Leśnieswki's work on the theory of definition may occasion howls of protest, that their requirements only concern formal language, that I am trying to straitjacket the freedom of natural languages, and so on. I reply that the protest and the whole position which goes with it concedes at once too much and too little to formal languages. It concedes too much in apparently supposing that natural languages resemble formal languages in being in some sense *theories*. But this absurd. What axioms and principles do I have to know and accept, and on pain of aphasia refuse to give up, in order to qualify as a speaker of English? None. But if there are none then nothing in my understanding of the English word 'person' dictates to me what I must suppose the criteria of personal identity to be. And I cannot read anything off from my understanding of the notion if nothing is written there. English is not a theory, and it never will be. But the objection also concedes far too little to formalization. What after all is formalizability? It is surely not a substantial or extra requirement over and above the coherence and coherent extensibility of a set of beliefs that they be formalizable. If the beliefs and the concepts of English speakers systematically resisted codification might that not show there was something wrong with what we do? And if our practices do not systematically resist codification then surely what we do is formalizable. On the other hand, if what English speakers do is not formalizable that suggests a rather deep-seated incoherence of some kind. There is not a shred of evidence, however, that we are incoherent in this way. If so, formalization is possible after all, and it may still help us to see where we believe *particular* incompatible things. It will do English no harm if we stop believing them and become consistent. Nor, since English is not a theory, would it standardly *change* English if we stopped believing incompatible things. (As will transpire, however, I do not think we do believe incompatible things about persons and their identies.)

⁵² A. J. Ayer 'The Problem of Knowledge', p. 196 (Penguin Books, Harmondsworth, Middlesex 1956). See also Williams' 'Personal Identity and Individuation', op. cit. (Note 47 above).

⁵³ See 'Physicalism', *Philosophical Review*, July 1965.

⁵⁴ Thomas Reid 'Essays on the Intellectual Powers of Man' (ed. A. D. Woozley, London, 1941) quoted by Sidney Shoemaker *Self Knowledge and Self-Identity* (Cornell University Press 1963), Chapter One, where see also pp. 246 and 258.

⁵⁵ There is an argument of Bishop Butler's which might be supposed to obstruct this approach. (Cp. Williams and Ayer, cited footnote 52 above).

But though consciousness of what is past does thus ascertain our personal identity to ourselves, yet to say that it makes personal identity, or is necessary to our being the same persons, is to say that a person has not existed a single moment, nor done one action but what he can remember; indeed none but what he reflects upon. And one should really think it self-evident, that consciousness of personal identity presupposes, and therefore cannot constitute, personal identity; any more than knowledge, in any other case, can constitute truth which it presupposes.   (First Dissertation to the *Analogy of Religion*)

The first point is quite ineffective against the view that a *sufficiency* of experience-memory is a prerequisite of being a person. The second point is more threatening, however. It might be held to show that such experience-memory cannot be relevant to the principle of individuation for persons because a principle of individuation for persons would have to *pre-exist* the formulation of any memory requirement for plenary personhood; the requirement would have to stipulate sufficient memory of *his* past history and *his* experiences. But I do not think the point is as powerful as it looks. [See also Appendix 5.6]

It must surely be possible to define a certain kind K of machines by specifying two features of K-machine operation—:

(*a*) a K can punch tickets which are presented to it,

(*b*) a K punches a ticket only if it has not punched it before, and it reports to the superintendent the second and illicit presentation of any ticket.

Now if the Butler argument were correct then it would have to be absurd to contend that the addition of (b) could make any difference to the principle of individuation for Ks. That would have to have been settled already by the time condition (a) was completed. The objection would continue that if (b) added anything to what (a) determined about identity-conditions for Ks then it could only import the possibility of contradiction or the quite unacceptable possibility of a case of R (see 1.2).

To see the implausibility of this argument it is enough to consider the situation in which a number of Ks are disassembled into punching-components (or (a)-components) and memory-cum-reporting-components (or (b)-components). Suppose Ks consist only of (a)- and (b)-components interlocked, and that components are exchanged between several of the Ks. The Butler argument would then tell us that it was *incoherent* to decide to individuate Ks by their memory-components. Now it may not be mandatory to decide the matter this way nor compulsory to decide to say that some of the K-machines were fitted with new or different (a)-components. But it is surely not an *incoherent* decision.

I think the Butler argument has to make the illicit supposition that the definition of K proceeds by picking out a subclass of machines which obey condition (a) and then picking out a sub-subclass which obey both conditions (a) and (b). But this need not be so. *Machine* itself is a quite dubious sortal. It is hardly better than *thing*. And condition (a) itself need not be construed as *completing* the specification of a genuine sortal which will then await further restriction by (b). Conditions (a) and (b) can be understood together as *jointly* defining a kind K. Neither need be understood in this context as *by itself* defining any sortal at all. The cross reference is then harmless and the account of K-machines can even be extended by a stipulation that the (b)- component 'dominates' the (a)-component so far as individuation is concerned.

The example is very trivial but it suggests a model for a more complicated and harmlessly cross-referential specification of an ordered hierarchy of functions of persons: sentience, desire, character, factual memory . . . , the whole succession dominated by experience memory. It also suggests an interesting conceptual truth about memory, or about remembering X-ing; which I shall take to be a necessarily *enmattered* capacity whose genesis must be causally dependent on the parcel which possesses the capacity having X-ed, and whose existence must be causally responsible for the possessor's recalling his X-ing. These necessities derive respectively from the fact that it is of the nature of memory to be something which can be reactivated after long disuse, and from the fact that it is of the nature of memory for its exercise to be in principle distinguishable from the fluke narration of past events such as X-ing. If this is right then any correct account of individuation through memory is already deeply involved with matter. But the K-machine example enables us to see one more way in which it is so involved. For a K-machine with a new punching-component to 'remember' punching a ticket the punching-component need not be the same as the original puncher. But the memory component itself must have been part of a *whole* machine which punched that ticket. The memory-component must have been *there*. Similarly then a parcel of matter which is a person must have its memory imprinted on *it*. And this is a conceptual truth. But then there cannot be 'exchange of memory' without exchange of matter between parcels. And it will be maintained here that this is not exchange of memory. It is rather the exchange by two core-persons of individuatively inessential matter. (Nothing which is said here is meant to rule out the gradual *repair* of a memory provided there is a unique spatio-temporal path for the organized parcel on which the memory is imprinted.)

[56] For present purposes I ignore his doctrine of separable intellect.

[57] See generally *Metaphysics* Z.VI.1031^{a13}–1032^{a12} and 1037^{a7-8}, 1036^{a16}f, and 104^{b32-4}.

[58]Aristotle would insistently repudiate this whole line of argument and he has a number of special defences against it.

In the first place he has a doctrine which enables him to say that the blunted axe and the decaying human body are in any case an axe and a body only *homonymously*. This is a doctrine which it is perhaps more important to understand than to reiterate. (See footnote 61 and the discussion of *Met.* 1035^{b14}, Cp. also *Met.* 1044^{b35}).

In the second place Aristotle might seem to have a rather straightforward way of denying that the soul is the living body (cp. *De Anima* 414^{a20}) and of justifying that denial. For in spite of his assertion that soul is substance, Aristotle gives the form of axe as *chopping* and that of eye as *seeing* (412^{b18} following). These are concepts whose understanding is certainly a condition of understanding *axe* or *eye*. They come to much the same as *being an axe* or *being an eye*, but they are not strictly the same concepts as the concepts *axe* and *eye*. It might then be said that Kallias' soul, if it is to be seen in parallel with *this axe's form*, is strictly some kind of universal. It will only be the analogue of what *makes* this particular axe an axe. But this plea cannot block the difficulties we have been raising. We have only to ask what it is that can correspond to the universal *psūchē* as some particular *axe* corresponds to the universal *being an axe*. There is an f such that in virtue of *psūchē* Kallias is a particular f. What value can f take? *Chopping* makes this an *axe*. Psūchē makes Kallias a *what*? If f gives the answer then we shall expect to be able to count under f and reidentify fs. (*Entelecheiai*, fully realized substances, and particular *suntheta*, complexes of matter and form, are surely canonical examples of things one can count and reidentify and so on. And note that *psūchē* is *entelecheia* and a *suntheton*.) If the answer to the question be that the particular f is a particular *empsūchon* (alive thing), we must ask 'alive *what*?'. If this receives the difficult answer *body* it can only raise the problem mentioned in the text. If the answer be *man* that is fine, but if the form *axe* makes this particular axe this *axe*, surely *psūchē* makes Kallias this particular *psūchē*. And for Kallias then, *psūchē* and *man* must come to the same. The resolution which I shall offer Aristotle is precisely this—that the particular f is *this particular psūchē* or, equally good, *this particular man*. But he must then follow me into an investigation of the general continuity and persistence conditions for any psūchē, distinguish them as I do from the conditions for a body, and give up speaking of Kallias *having* a soul. He is one. (Cp. *Met.* 1037^{a9}).

⁵⁹ See Note 44.

⁶⁰ See Note 55 and op. cit., pp. 20, 23–25, 30, 193–4, 231, 245–247.

⁶¹ In case I seem to have stretched belief to breaking point in making this claim for Aristotle I shall here vindicate it by reference to *Metaphysics* Z 1035^{b25} and — 1024^{a24}. One preliminary explanation is necessary.

Aristotle holds that the material parts of a thing are, in general, logically posterior to the thing. But there is another kind of part, a part in the sense of what figures in the explanation of what a thing is. Such parts as these are components of the definition of the thing (or, as I should rather say, they figure in the explanation of the sortal concept under which the thing falls) and they are not posterior but prior to the thing. Now the reason why the material parts of x, p, are accounted posterior to x by Aristotle seems to be something like this. Suppose we take the example of parts of the body. They have to be picked out or individuated in some way or other, and any correct way of picking them out will have to make clear *what* exactly we are picking out. But this involves making clear the existence and persistence conditions (for Aristotle slightly peculiar) of the bodily parts we do pick out (cp. 3.2 above). These can only be entirely correctly given if we pick these parts out *as parts of this or that living body*. (That anyway is Aristotle's view of bodily parts. For him such are really living-bodily-parts. The generalizable point is that the picking out of p must *somehow* make clear what p are. See 3.2.) So Aristotle writes:

> 'And the finger is defined by the whole body. For a finger is a particular kind of part of a man. Thus such parts as are material, and into which the whole is resolved as into matter, are posterior to the whole; but such as are parts in the sense of parts of the formula and of the essence as expressed in the formula [*tou logou kai tēs ousias tēs kata ton logon*], are prior. Either all or some of them.' (Metaphysics 1035^b following, trans. Tredennick.)

But a peculiar confluence of the two notions of part can and does arise for parts of the soul, when it is remembered that these are also bodily parts. For although the actual enmattered parts of a man's living body are posterior to the living body as a whole, nevertheless considering them schematically and *functionally* the conceptual requirement for a part with this role and a part with that role was already present and built into the definition of what a man is. For the account of his *psūchē*, his faculties and form of life, can be conceptually delineated in advance of biological discoveries.

> 'Now the soul of an animal (which is the substance of the living creature) is its substance, it is what the animal by definition is, the form or essence of a certain particular kind of body; and every part of this soul which is properly defined will be defined by its function, sensation being the one functional prerequisite to all other functions. It follows that the parts of the soul (which have this functional definition as well as a particular material realization) are prior, some or all of them, to any particular concrete animal embodied in any particular matter. And it is the same for each particular animal. Now the material body and its material parts are posterior to the essence [the soul which they embody or realize] and it is not the essence [what it is to be a soul] but a concrete embodiment of the essence, a particular enmattered soul, which can be disassembled into these particular material parts. So there is a way in which the parts of the body are posterior and a way in which they are prior to the concrete individual soul. Being what they are, living-bodily-parts, they cannot even continue as what they are, so cannot exist, after severance from the body. A finger in any old state is not strictly a finger. A dead finger is only a finger by

courtesy, equivocally. But there are some parts which are neither prior nor posterior but logically simultaneous with the *psūchē* itself, *such as are conceptually indispensable to its existence (kuria) and in which the whole formula itself, the essential substance, is immediately present (en hoi protoi ho logos kai hē ousia), e.g. perhaps the heart or the brain.* It does not matter here which it is.' (1035^{b14} following, paraphrased.)

This or that particular bodily part, p, can be individuated as part of this particular whole living-body or *psūchē*. Thus p is posterior. But it was already a conceptual element in the description of the life and faculties which define this kind of *psūchē* that something would have to play p's role. Taken so, described simply as the thing that plays that role, p is prior. But we cannot say of the brain or heart that it is prior or posterior. It cannot be prior to the *psūchē* because its functional mission embraces *everything* which is integral to the *psūchē* itself, and functionally speaking its role is causally integral to the very persistence of life itself. For the same reason it cannot be posterior. For it is not then individuated in essential dependence on the living-body. It is itself the individuative nucleus of the composite living-body.

The importance of the 1035^b passage, both in the explanation of Aristotle's localization of the psūchē (cp. 703^{a28-b2} *De Motu Animalium* and 670^{a23} *De Partibus Animalium*) and in the refutation of Nuyens' disastrous attempt to remove this feature from the hylomorphic doctrine, has been emphasized by Irving Block 'The Order of Aristotle's Psychological Writings', *American Journal of Philology* Jan. 1961, vol. LXXXII no. 235, and by W. F. R. Hardie, 'Aristotle's Treatment of the Relation between Body and Soul'. *Philosophical Quarterly*, Vol. 14, no. 54, 1964.

[62] J. S. Griffith 'The Neural Basis of Conscious Decision', Inaugural Lecture, 27 October 1966, to be published by Bedford College, London.

[63] *New English Dictionary* Oxford 1933 (Supplement, page 207). '*Clone* [ad. Gr. κλών twig, slip]. A group of cultivated plants the individuals of which are transplanted parts of one original seedling or stock, the propagation having been carried out by the use of grafts, cuttings, bulbs, etc. . . .' The following is cited (1903). 'The clons of apples, pears, strawberries, etc., do not propagate true to seed, while this is one of the most important characters of races of wheat and corn.'

The passage from pages 23-4 of Sydney Shoemaker's book *Self Knowledge and Self Identity* is used by permission of Cornell University Press, © 1963 by Cornell University. The example on page 43 was suggested to me by Miss Hidé Ishiguro.

INDEX

References to the text are mostly by page, to footnotes by number (e.g.: fn. 47), to Appendix by section number (e.g.: Appx. 5.3). The index is selective with respect to some names (e.g. Aristotle) and some topics (e.g. Sortal, Leibniz' Law). But most of the examples much discussed have been given an index-entry under some short label.